Practical Java: Build Real-World Applications with Java

A Step-by-Step Guide to Creating Full-Scale Java Applications

BOOZMAN RICHARD

BOOKER BLUNT

Table of Content

TABLE OF CONTENTS

INTRODUCTION

Practical Java: Build Real-World Applications with Java

Java has long been one of the most powerful and versatile programming languages in the world. Known for its **platform independence, robust ecosystem,** and **extensive community support,** Java continues to be the language of choice for building large-scale applications across industries. Whether you're developing enterprise-grade applications, working with big data, building mobile apps, or integrating with cloud services, Java offers a wealth of tools, frameworks, and libraries to meet your needs.

This book, **"Practical Java: Build Real-World Applications with Java",** is designed to take both beginner and experienced Java developers on a comprehensive journey through the fundamentals, best practices, and advanced techniques necessary to build practical, high-performance Java applications. Whether you're just starting with Java or looking to deepen your knowledge of the language and its ecosystem, this book provides clear, real-world examples to help you succeed in today's rapidly evolving development landscape.

Why This Book?

In today's competitive software development environment, it's not enough to just know how to write Java code. Developers need to understand how to structure applications, optimize performance, manage cloud integrations, and apply industry best practices to ensure that their code is scalable, maintainable, and efficient. This book is not just about learning syntax or basic programming concepts; it's about **building real-world, enterprise-level applications** that can handle complex requirements and large user bases.

Here's why this book stands out:

- **Real-World Application Focus**: This book emphasizes building practical applications that can be deployed in production environments. Each chapter is designed to give you hands-on experience with building Java applications for real use cases— whether it's building microservices, integrating with cloud platforms, or designing scalable databases.
- **Comprehensive Coverage**: You'll not only learn the basics of Java but also advanced topics such as **cloud integration, big data processing, microservices architecture**, and **performance**

7

optimization. The book covers every aspect of Java development, from building APIs to using design patterns, ensuring you gain a well-rounded skill set.

- **Best Practices and Industry Standards**: We emphasize writing clean, maintainable code using the best industry practices. By following the guidance in this book, you'll learn how to write code that is readable, scalable, and ready for enterprise-level deployment.

- **Forward-Looking Content**: With **Java's continuous evolution**, including developments in **Project Loom**, **cloud-native applications**, and **AI/Big Data** integrations, this book keeps you up-to-date with the latest trends and prepares you for the future of Java development.

What Will You Learn?

This book is divided into 27 chapters, each focused on a specific aspect of Java development. Here's what you can expect to learn throughout the book:

1. **Java Fundamentals**: The book starts with the core concepts of Java programming, including data types, control flow, methods, and object-oriented

programming. These chapters will help you build a solid foundation in Java.

2. **Building Java Applications**: As you progress, we dive into practical topics such as building APIs, interacting with databases, and using Java for web and desktop applications. We focus on **real-world applications** that are relevant to the modern Java developer.

3. **Advanced Java Development**: We then move into advanced topics, such as **microservices architecture**, **cloud integration**, and **performance optimization**. You will gain the knowledge and tools required to build high-performing, scalable applications that can run in the cloud or handle massive datasets.

4. **Design Patterns and Best Practices**: We cover essential **design patterns** (e.g., **Singleton**, **Factory**, **Observer**) and **best practices** for writing clean, maintainable code. These patterns help you design software that is modular, scalable, and easy to understand.

5. **Future-Proofing Your Java Skills**: As Java continues to evolve, we explore how to keep your skills up-to-date, including the use of **Project Loom**,

9

cloud services, big data technologies, and Java's growing role in fields like **AI** and **machine learning**.

Target Audience

This book is intended for:

- **Beginner Java developers**: If you're new to Java, this book provides a solid foundation to get started with writing and deploying Java applications. Each chapter builds on the previous one, so you can steadily increase your knowledge and skills.

- **Experienced Java developers**: If you're already familiar with Java but want to take your skills to the next level, this book covers advanced topics such as **microservices architecture**, **cloud computing**, and **performance optimization**. You'll also learn about Java's latest innovations, including **Project Loom** and its impact on concurrency.

- **Software engineers**: If you work in Java and want to design scalable, maintainable applications using modern tools and frameworks, this book gives you the knowledge needed to build enterprise-grade solutions.

What Makes This Book Different?

- **Practical Focus**: While many Java books cover theory, this one places emphasis on **practical development**. Each concept you learn is immediately applied to real-world scenarios, ensuring that you are ready to build production-ready applications.

- **Hands-On Examples**: Throughout the book, you'll find hands-on examples that walk you through how to solve common development challenges. From **API design** to **cloud deployment**, the examples are based on actual industry use cases.

- **Clear, Actionable Steps**: Each chapter presents clear instructions and step-by-step guidance, allowing you to follow along easily and implement what you've learned in your own projects.

Structure of the Book

The book is divided into several sections that progress logically from beginner to advanced topics:

- **Section 1**: **Java Basics**: Covers the fundamental building blocks of Java programming.

11

- **Section 2**: **Building Java Applications**: Focuses on application development using Java, including web services and APIs.
- **Section 3**: **Advanced Topics**: Introduces complex topics like microservices, cloud computing, and big data processing.
- **Section 4**: **Best Practices and Performance Optimization**: Covers important Java development techniques, design patterns, and performance optimization strategies.
- **Section 5**: **The Future of Java**: Discusses Java's future role in cloud computing, AI, and big data.

Conclusion

Whether you are a **beginner** looking to understand the core principles of Java, or an **experienced developer** aiming to master advanced topics like **microservices** and **cloud-native applications**, this book is designed to equip you with the knowledge and skills to thrive in the world of Java development. **"Practical Java: Build Real-World Applications with Java"** will guide you through every step of the process, from writing clean, efficient code to deploying your Java applications to the cloud, ensuring that you are prepared for the future of Java development.

As you progress through the chapters, you'll be building **real-world applications**, applying the best practices of modern Java development, and staying on top of emerging trends. Whether you're working on your first Java project or preparing for your next big enterprise-level application, this book will serve as an invaluable resource, preparing you for success in the dynamic field of Java development.

CHAPTER 1

INTRODUCTION TO CONTAINERIZATION

What is Containerization?

Containerization is a method of packaging software so that it can run uniformly and consistently across different computing environments. Think of it as a way to bundle an application along with its dependencies—libraries, configurations, and other necessary tools—into a single, portable unit known as a **container**. This container can then run on any machine that supports container technology, regardless of the underlying operating system or hardware.

Unlike traditional virtualization, which involves running an entire operating system along with the application, containers only package the application and its dependencies, making them lightweight and fast. This allows developers to create, test, and deploy applications in isolated environments that can be easily shared across various systems, ensuring that the application works exactly the same everywhere.

Why Containerization is Essential for Modern Apps

Containerization has become a cornerstone for modern application development because it addresses several challenges that developers face today:

1. **Portability**: Containers make it possible to package an application with all its dependencies and run it consistently on any machine or cloud platform. This eliminates the "works on my machine" problem, where an app runs on one developer's machine but fails on another due to different configurations.

2. **Scalability**: Containers can be easily scaled up or down to meet changing demand. Whether you need to add more resources for high-traffic periods or scale down to save costs, containers allow for efficient, automated scaling.

3. **Faster Deployment**: Containers enable faster development cycles. Developers can quickly build and test applications within containers, leading to shorter release cycles and quicker iterations on new features.

4. **Isolation**: Each container operates in isolation, meaning that the application within the container does not affect the host system or other containers. This makes containers ideal for running microservices or any applications that need to be maintained separately.

5. **Efficiency**: Containers share the host system's kernel, which makes them more lightweight compared to

traditional virtual machines. This reduces overhead, improves resource usage, and leads to better performance and faster boot times.

6. **Consistency Across Environments**: Containers ensure that the application behaves the same way from development to staging to production. This removes inconsistencies caused by environmental differences, ensuring better stability and predictability.

Key Benefits of Docker in the Development Lifecycle

Docker has gained massive popularity due to its ability to simplify containerization. Here's why Docker stands out:

1. **Simplifies Setup and Configuration**: Docker makes it easy to set up and configure containers. With Docker, you can define the entire environment, including dependencies, libraries, and system tools, in a `Dockerfile`. This can then be shared and executed on any machine, ensuring consistent environments.

2. **Easy Version Control for Containers**: Docker images can be versioned, tagged, and stored in registries like Docker Hub or private repositories. This allows developers to maintain different versions of their application and easily roll back or deploy new versions.

3. **Integration with CI/CD Pipelines**: Docker integrates seamlessly into continuous integration and continuous deployment (CI/CD) workflows. This allows for automated testing, building, and deployment, streamlining the development pipeline.

4. **Isolation for Microservices**: Docker makes it easy to run microservices architectures. Each service can run in its own container, ensuring that they don't interfere with each other, and allowing for faster updates and scaling.

5. **Cross-platform Compatibility**: Docker containers can run on any platform—Linux, macOS, or Windows. This cross-platform compatibility makes Docker an attractive solution for teams working in mixed environments.

6. **Resource Efficiency**: Docker is lightweight compared to traditional virtual machines. It uses fewer system resources because it doesn't require a full OS to run multiple applications, resulting in improved performance and reduced costs.

A Brief History of Docker and Its Ecosystem

Docker was first released in **March 2013** by **Solomon Hykes** and his team at a company called **dotCloud**. Initially, Docker was based on the idea of using **LXC (Linux Containers)**, a Linux-based virtualization technology, to enable developers to package applications and their dependencies into lightweight containers.

However, Docker quickly evolved into its own containerization platform, offering greater flexibility and ease of use than LXC.

By **2014**, Docker became a household name, and the company Docker, Inc. was formed. Docker's platform quickly gained adoption across the software development industry because it solved a number of pressing challenges related to consistency, scalability, and portability in application development.

Some key milestones in Docker's evolution include:

- **2013**: Docker's initial release, based on LXC.
- **2014**: The Docker engine became a more refined product, allowing for greater adoption in enterprise environments. Docker also introduced **Docker Hub**, a cloud-based registry for storing and sharing Docker images.
- **2015**: Docker introduced **Docker Compose**, enabling multi-container applications, and **Docker Swarm**, a clustering and orchestration tool for managing containers in large environments.
- **2017**: Docker launched **Docker for Windows** and **Docker for Mac**, making Docker accessible to non-Linux users.
- **2018**: Docker was increasingly integrated with cloud-native technologies, like Kubernetes, and Docker's container runtime engine became a critical part of the modern software stack.

Docker's ecosystem has grown rapidly, with numerous associated tools like **Docker Compose**, **Docker Swarm**, and **Docker Hub**, all of which are designed to make working with containers easier. As containerization became more widespread, Docker also integrated with orchestration systems like **Kubernetes**, which is used for managing large-scale containerized applications.

Summary:

In this chapter, we've introduced containerization and its importance for modern applications. We've explored the key benefits Docker brings to the development lifecycle, including portability, scalability, and consistency. Finally, we've traced the history of Docker, from its inception in 2013 to its widespread adoption today as a foundational tool for developers around the world. Docker's simplicity and power make it the ideal choice for anyone looking to adopt containerization and improve their application development workflows.

CHAPTER 2

SETTING UP DOCKER

Installing Docker on Different Systems (Linux, macOS, Windows)

Before you can start using Docker, you need to install it on your machine. Docker supports multiple operating systems, and the installation process varies slightly depending on whether you're using **Linux**, **macOS**, or **Windows**. Below are the installation steps for each system.

1. Installing Docker on Linux

Docker supports many distributions of Linux, including Ubuntu, CentOS, and Debian. Here's how to install Docker on a popular Linux distribution: **Ubuntu**.

- **Step 1: Update System Packages**

  Open a terminal and run the following command to ensure your system's packages are up to date:

  ```
  bash
  ```

  ```
  sudo apt-get update
  ```

- **Step 2: Install Required Dependencies**

  Docker requires a few dependencies to run. Install them by running:

  ```bash
  sudo apt-get install apt-transport-https
  ca-certificates curl software-properties-
  common
  ```

- **Step 3: Add Docker's Official GPG Key**

  Docker's packages are signed, and you need to add the official GPG key to your system to ensure the authenticity of the installation package:

  ```bash
  curl                            -fsSL
  https://download.docker.com/linux/ubuntu/
  gpg | sudo apt-key add -
  ```

- **Step 4: Add Docker Repository**

  Add Docker's official repository to your system:

  ```bash
  ```

21

```
sudo add-apt-repository "deb [arch=amd64]
https://download.docker.com/linux/ubuntu
$(lsb_release -cs) stable"
```

- **Step 5: Install Docker**

Now you can install Docker by running:

```
bash
```

```
sudo apt-get update
sudo apt-get install docker-ce
```

- **Step 6: Verify Installation**

Verify that Docker is installed and running with the following command:

```
bash
```

```
sudo systemctl status docker
```

You should see a message indicating that Docker is active and running.

2. Installing Docker on macOS

Docker Desktop is the recommended method for installing Docker on macOS. Here's how to install it:

- **Step 1: Download Docker Desktop for Mac**

  Go to the official Docker website and download the Docker Desktop for Mac.

- **Step 2: Install Docker Desktop**

  After downloading the `.dmg` file, double-click it to open the installer. Then drag the Docker application to the `Applications` folder.

- **Step 3: Launch Docker Desktop**

  Open Docker from your `Applications` folder. The first time you run Docker, you might be prompted to enter your system password to allow Docker to make changes to your system. Follow the prompts to complete the installation.

- **Step 4: Verify Installation**

  Once Docker is running, you can verify that it's working correctly by opening a terminal and typing:

```bash

docker --version
```

This will return the version of Docker installed on your system.

3. Installing Docker on Windows

Docker Desktop is also the easiest way to install Docker on Windows. Here's how to install it:

- **Step 1: Check Windows Version**

  Docker Desktop requires **Windows 10 Pro** or higher. If you are running Windows 10 Home, you will need to install **Windows Subsystem for Linux (WSL)** to use Docker.

- **Step 2: Download Docker Desktop for Windows**

  Go to the official Docker website and download Docker Desktop for Windows.

- **Step 3: Install Docker Desktop**

  After downloading the `.exe` file, double-click it to begin the installation. Follow the prompts to install Docker Desktop. You may need to enable Hyper-V and WSL 2 during the installation process if it's not already enabled.

- **Step 4: Restart Your Computer**

After installation, restart your computer to complete the setup.

- **Step 5: Verify Installation**

  Once Docker Desktop is running, open PowerShell or Command Prompt and run the following command to verify the installation:

  bash

  ```
  docker --version
  ```

  This will display the installed version of Docker.

Understanding Docker Desktop

Docker Desktop is a user-friendly interface that simplifies working with Docker containers and images. It's available for both **macOS** and **Windows**, and it allows you to manage your Docker environment using both a graphical interface and the command line. Here's what Docker Desktop provides:

- **Graphical Interface**: You can easily manage containers, images, and Docker settings through a visual interface. This is helpful for beginners who prefer not to work directly with the command line.

- **Docker CLI Integration**: Docker Desktop includes the Docker command-line interface (CLI), which you can use for more advanced control over containers and images.
- **Docker Compose**: Docker Desktop comes with Docker Compose pre-installed, allowing you to work with multi-container applications.
- **Automatic Updates**: Docker Desktop automatically checks for updates and installs them, ensuring you always have the latest version of Docker.
- **System Tray Integration**: Docker Desktop runs in the background, and you can interact with it directly from the system tray on Windows or the menu bar on macOS.

Verifying Installation and Running the First Docker Container

Once Docker is installed, you can verify that everything is set up correctly and run your first container:

- **Step 1: Verify Docker Installation**

  Open a terminal or command prompt and run:

  ```bash
  ```

  ```
  docker --version
  ```

This command will print the Docker version if the installation was successful.

- **Step 2: Run Your First Docker Container**

  Docker provides a simple way to test your installation by running a pre-built image. Run the following command to pull the **hello-world** image and start a container:

  ```bash
  docker run hello-world
  ```

  This command will download the **hello-world** image from Docker Hub (if it's not already on your machine), and then run it as a container. The output should display a message confirming that your installation is successful and that Docker is running properly.

- **Step 3: Inspect the Running Container**

  To inspect the container that was just started, use the following command to see a list of running containers:

  ```bash
  docker ps
  ```

27

This will display details about the containers that are currently running, such as the container ID, image name, and status.

- **Step 4: Stopping and Removing Containers**

If you want to stop the running container, use:

```bash

docker stop <container_id>
```

Replace `<container_id>` with the actual container ID that you obtained from the `docker ps` command.

To remove the container, use:

```bash

docker rm <container_id>
```

Summary:

In this chapter, we covered how to install Docker on different systems, including **Linux**, **macOS**, and **Windows**. We also explored Docker Desktop and its role in simplifying Docker management with a user-friendly interface. Finally, we ran our first Docker container to verify that the installation was successful. With Docker now set up, you're ready to begin exploring more advanced Docker features and workflows in the coming chapters!

CHAPTER 3

CORE CONCEPTS OF DOCKER

What Are Containers, Images, and Registries?

In Docker, the terms **containers**, **images**, and **registries** are fundamental concepts that every developer needs to understand. Let's break them down:

- **Containers**:

  A **container** is a lightweight, standalone, and executable package of software. It includes everything needed to run the software, such as the code, runtime, libraries, and system tools. Containers are isolated from the host system and other containers, which makes them ideal for running applications in a controlled and consistent environment.

  - Containers are **ephemeral**: they can be started, stopped, and deleted without affecting the underlying system or other containers.
  - Containers are based on **images** (discussed below) and run instances of these images.
- **Images**:

  A **Docker image** is a read-only template used to create containers. It's essentially a snapshot of the filesystem that contains the application and all its dependencies, such as libraries, binaries, configuration files, and the system tools required to run it.

- o Images are built using **Dockerfiles**, which define the configuration and dependencies required for the application.
- o When you run a container, you are running an instance of an image.

- **Registries**:

  A **Docker registry** is a repository for storing and distributing Docker images. It's like a database for Docker images where images are uploaded and pulled from.

  - o The most common registry is **Docker Hub**, which is public and contains thousands of pre-built images for common software.
  - o You can also create private registries for storing custom or proprietary images that you want to keep secure or share within your organization.

Docker Hub, the default public registry, provides a convenient place to find and download Docker images, but you can also use private registries to store and manage your own custom-built images.

Docker Architecture: Docker Engine, Daemon, and CLI

Understanding Docker's architecture is key to grasping how Docker functions under the hood. Docker is composed of several components that work together to create, manage, and run containers.

- **Docker   Engine**:
  The **Docker Engine** is the core part of Docker that is responsible for running containers. It can be thought of as the **runtime** for Docker and is made up of several components:
  - o **Docker   Daemon   (dockerd)**:
    The **Docker Daemon** is the background service that manages Docker containers, images, and networks. It listens for Docker API requests and handles the lifecycle of containers. It can run on your local machine or on remote servers.
  - o **Docker CLI (Command-Line Interface)**:
    The **Docker CLI** is the command-line tool that allows you to interact with the Docker Daemon. It provides the commands you use to create and manage Docker containers, images, networks, and volumes. Commands like `docker run`, `docker ps`, and `docker build` are examples of how you interact with the Docker Daemon through the CLI.

- o **Docker**   **API**:
  The **Docker API** allows you to interact programmatically with Docker, enabling automation and integration with other software systems.

The Docker Engine handles the execution of containers, while the Docker CLI lets you issue commands to manage those containers. The Docker Daemon does the heavy lifting by creating, running, and maintaining containers based on your instructions.

Containers vs. Virtual Machines

One common question that arises when working with Docker is how containers differ from **virtual machines (VMs)**. Although both containers and VMs provide isolated environments for running applications, they work very differently and offer distinct advantages and trade-offs.

- **Virtual Machines (VMs)**: A **virtual machine** is a full operating system (OS) that runs on top of a physical machine via a hypervisor. Each VM includes the entire OS along with the application and necessary dependencies, which makes VMs relatively heavy and resource-intensive.

33

- o VMs require a hypervisor to manage them, adding an additional layer of overhead.
- o VMs can take several minutes to start because the OS must boot up each time.
- o They are often larger in size (several gigabytes) due to the full OS and overhead.

- **Containers**: Containers, on the other hand, share the host machine's OS kernel but run in isolated user spaces. This makes them lightweight and fast to start compared to VMs. Containers only include the application and its dependencies, not the full OS.
  - o Containers are much faster to start, often taking only a few seconds.
  - o They are lightweight and require less memory, often taking up megabytes rather than gigabytes.
  - o Containers use the host OS kernel, which allows for faster boot times and less overhead.

Key Differences:

- **Isolation**: Containers are isolated at the application level, while VMs are isolated at the system level.
- **Performance**: Containers are generally more efficient because they don't require a full operating system.
- **Resource Usage**: Containers are much lighter and consume fewer resources compared to VMs, which need their own OS and associated resources.

How Docker Makes Applications Portable

One of the biggest advantages of Docker is its ability to make applications **highly portable**. Let's explore how Docker achieves this:

- **Consistent   Environment**: Docker containers encapsulate all the dependencies, libraries, and environment settings required to run an application. This means that if an application runs successfully inside a Docker container on a developer's local machine, it will behave the same way when deployed to a staging environment or a production server.

- **Cross-Platform   Compatibility**: Docker ensures that containers can run on any machine, regardless of the underlying operating system. Docker containers abstract away differences between OS distributions, which means developers don't have to worry about compatibility issues when moving applications between different environments (e.g., from local development machines to cloud servers or from Linux to Windows).

- **Portability   Across   Cloud   Providers**: Docker containers are platform-agnostic, meaning they can be deployed to any cloud environment (AWS, Azure, Google Cloud, etc.). This portability allows developers to

35

build once and deploy anywhere without worrying about vendor lock-in.

- **Versioned** **Images**: Docker images can be versioned, meaning you can track and control the versions of your application. If an image works in one environment, you can be confident it will work in other environments as long as the same image is used. This makes it easier to move applications between different stages of development, testing, and production.

- **Simplified** **Deployment**: Since containers are portable, deploying an application in Docker is often as simple as running a `docker run` command. Whether you are deploying to a local machine or a cloud server, Docker makes deployment straightforward and predictable.

Summary:

In this chapter, we've covered the core concepts of Docker, starting with the key building blocks: **containers**, **images**, and **registries**. We also explored Docker's architecture, including the **Docker Engine**, **Daemon**, and **CLI**. Additionally, we compared **containers vs. virtual machines**, highlighting the differences in isolation, performance, and resource usage. Finally, we discussed how Docker makes applications portable by ensuring consistent environments, cross-platform compatibility, and simplified deployment across different systems and cloud providers. These concepts lay the foundation for understanding how Docker works and why it's a game-changer for modern application development.

CHAPTER 4

DOCKER IMAGES AND CONTAINERS EXPLAINED

How Docker Images Are Built and Stored

In Docker, **images** are the blueprints or templates used to create containers. An image contains all the files, libraries, dependencies, and instructions needed to run an application. These images are built from a **Dockerfile**, a simple text file that defines everything the image needs to function.

Building Docker Images

Docker images are built using the `docker build` command, which reads the instructions in a `Dockerfile` and packages them into an image. Here's how the process works:

1. **Create a Dockerfile**:
   The `Dockerfile` is a text document that contains a series of instructions for Docker to execute. A basic Dockerfile might look like this:

   `Dockerfile`

```
# Use an official Python runtime as a base
image
FROM python:3.9-slim

# Set the working directory in the
container
WORKDIR /app

# the current directory contents into the
container
 . /app

# Install any dependencies
RUN pip install -r requirements.txt

# Make port 80 available to the outside
world
EXPOSE 80

# Define environment variable
ENV NAME World

# Run the application
CMD ["python", "app.py"]
```

This Dockerfile defines the following:

o The base image (FROM python:3.9-slim) —
   an official Python image.

- o A working directory within the container (`WORKDIR /app`).
- o ing application files into the container (`. /app`).
- o Installing dependencies (`RUN pip install -r requirements.txt`).
- o Exposing a port (`EXPOSE 80`) for communication.
- o Running a command to start the application (`CMD ["python", "app.py"]`).

2. **Build the Docker Image**: After you have your `Dockerfile`, use the `docker build` command to create the image:

```bash

docker build -t my-python-app .
```

The `-t` flag tags the image with a name (`my-python-app`). The period (`.`) tells Docker to build the image from the current directory.

3. **Verify the Image**: Once the image is built, you can list your images using:

```bash

docker images
```

This will show all images on your local machine, including the one you just built.

Storing Docker Images

Once an image is built, it can be stored and shared. Docker images are typically stored in a **Docker registry**. The most common registry is **Docker Hub**, but you can also create your own private registries.

- **Docker   Hub**:
  Docker Hub is a cloud-based registry service where developers can find and share container images. It contains a vast repository of pre-built images for everything from web servers to databases.
- **Private   Registries**:
  You can create a private Docker registry for storing your custom images securely. This is useful for teams that need to share proprietary applications or for keeping sensitive images private.

To push your image to Docker Hub, you must first tag it:

bash

```
docker tag my-python-app username/my-python-app
```

Then, push it to Docker Hub:

41

```bash
```

```
docker push username/my-python-app
```

This makes the image available on Docker Hub for other developers or systems to pull and use.

Understanding the Difference Between Containers and Images

It's essential to understand the distinction between **containers** and **images** in Docker. While both are closely related, they serve different purposes.

- **Docker Images**:
    - **Read-only**: Images are static and do not change. They are built using a `Dockerfile` and serve as the template for creating containers.
    - **Reusable**: Once an image is built, it can be reused across different systems and environments. You can pull images from a registry and use them to run containers on any machine.
    - **No state**: An image does not have any running state. It's simply a snapshot of the application and its dependencies.
- **Docker Containers**:
    - **Writable and dynamic**: Containers are instances of images that can be started, stopped, and

42

modified. Unlike images, containers are **read-write** and can have changes made to them during their execution.

- o **Ephemeral**: Containers are designed to be temporary and lightweight. When a container is stopped and removed, all changes made to it are lost (unless persistent storage is configured).

- o **Running instance of an image**: A container is a running instance of a Docker image. You can have multiple containers running from the same image, each with its own state and configuration.

In summary:

- Images are static, reusable templates.
- Containers are dynamic, running instances of images.

Creating Your First Docker Container from an Image

Now that you understand images and containers, let's create and run your first Docker container.

Step 1: Choose an Image from Docker Hub

Docker Hub has thousands of pre-built images that you can use to create containers. Let's use the popular `nginx` image as an example, which is a web server.

43

Step 2: Run a Docker Container

To run the `nginx` container, use the following command:

```bash
docker run -d -p 8080:80 --name my-nginx-container nginx
```

This command does the following:

- **-d**: Runs the container in detached mode (in the background).
- **-p 8080:80**: Maps port 8080 on the host to port 80 in the container.
- **--name my-nginx-container**: Assigns a name to the container.
- **nginx**: Specifies the image to use (in this case, the official `nginx` image from Docker Hub).

Once the container is running, you can access the `nginx` server by visiting `http://localhost:8080` in your web browser.

Step 3: Inspect the Running Container

You can check the status of your running container using:

```bash
```

44

```
docker ps
```

This will display the running container's details, such as container ID, image name, status, and port mappings.

Step 4: Stop and Remove the Container

When you're done, you can stop the container with:

```bash
bash
```

```
docker stop my-nginx-container
```

To remove the container:

```bash
bash
```

```
docker rm my-nginx-container
```

Docker Hub and Custom Image Creation

While Docker Hub provides thousands of pre-built images, you might need to create and share your own custom images.

Creating a Custom Image

To create a custom image, you first write a `Dockerfile` as shown in a previous section. After creating the `Dockerfile`, build the image using:

```bash
```

```
docker build -t my-custom-image .
```

This command will create a custom image with the tag `my-custom-image`.

Pushing Custom Images to Docker Hub

Once your custom image is ready, you can push it to Docker Hub (or any other registry) for others to use:

1. **Tag the Image**: Before pushing to Docker Hub, you need to tag your image with your Docker Hub username:

   ```bash
   ```

   ```
   docker tag my-custom-image username/my-custom-image
   ```

2. **Push the Image**:

   ```bash
   ```

   ```
   docker push username/my-custom-image
   ```

Now, anyone can pull your custom image by running:

```bash
```

```
docker pull username/my-custom-image
```

Summary:

In this chapter, we explored the core concepts behind Docker images and containers. We discussed how Docker images are built from a `Dockerfile`, stored in registries like Docker Hub, and used to create containers. We also compared containers and images, explaining the differences between the two. Finally, we walked through creating a container from an image and shared how to push your custom Docker images to Docker Hub for reuse. This sets the stage for understanding more advanced Docker features and workflows in the upcoming chapters.

CHAPTER 5

MANAGING DOCKER CONTAINERS

Starting, Stopping, and Restarting Containers

Once you have built a Docker image, you can create and manage containers from that image. Containers can be started, stopped, and restarted at any time, giving you full control over their lifecycle. Here's how you can manage container states:

Starting Containers

To run a container from an image, you can use the `docker run` command. This command not only starts a container but also creates it from the specified image. If the image is not found locally, Docker will download it from the registry.

Example:

```bash
docker run -d --name my-container nginx
```

This command will:

48

- Start a container in **detached mode** (-d), meaning it runs in the background.
- Name the container my-container.
- Use the nginx image to create and run the container.

Stopping Containers

To stop a running container, use the docker stop command, followed by the container's name or ID.

Example:

```bash
```

```
docker stop my-container
```

This will send a signal to the container to stop running. The container's processes will be gracefully terminated.

Restarting Containers

To restart a stopped container, you can use the docker restart command. This will stop the container and immediately start it again.

Example:

```bash
```

```
docker restart my-container
```

This command is useful when you need to apply changes or reinitialize a container without having to recreate it.

Container Lifecycle Management (Pause, Unpause, Remove)

Docker containers have a variety of lifecycle management options beyond just starting and stopping. These include pausing, unpausing, and removing containers.

Pausing a Container

Pausing a container will temporarily stop its processes without completely shutting down the container. This is useful if you want to freeze a container for later resumption without losing its state.

To pause a running container:

```bash
bash
```

```
docker pause my-container
```

This will pause all processes running inside the container.

Unpausing a Container

To resume a paused container, use the `docker unpause` command. This will allow the container's processes to continue running from where they left off.

Example:

```bash

docker unpause my-container
```

This will unpause the container and allow its processes to continue.

Removing a Container

When you're finished with a container, and you no longer need it, you can remove it. Stopped containers are not automatically deleted, so you must manually remove them to free up system resources.

To remove a stopped container:

```bash

docker rm my-container
```

This command removes the container, freeing up any resources it was using. Note that you can't remove a running container without stopping it first.

If you want to remove a container forcefully, even if it's running, use the -f flag:

```bash

docker rm -f my-container
```

This will stop and remove the container in one step.

Viewing Logs and Debugging Container Issues

Sometimes, containers may encounter issues during execution, and it's important to view logs or debug the container to diagnose problems.

Viewing Container Logs

Docker provides a powerful logging system that allows you to view the output from the container's running processes. This is useful for troubleshooting and debugging.

To view the logs of a specific container, use the docker logs command:

```
bash
```

```
docker logs my-container
```

This will show you the standard output (stdout) and standard error (stderr) from the container. If the container has been running for a while, the logs will include everything that has been printed to the console, including errors and debug messages.

If you want to follow the logs in real-time (similar to the `tail -f` command), you can use the `-f` flag:

```
bash
```

```
docker logs -f my-container
```

This will continuously display the log output as new entries are added.

Debugging Containers with `docker exec`

In some cases, you may need to interact directly with a container's environment to debug an issue. You can do this by using the `docker exec` command to run commands inside a running container.

Example: To get an interactive shell inside the container:

```
bash
```

```
docker exec -it my-container /bin/bash
```

This will open a Bash shell inside the container, allowing you to execute commands as if you were logged into the container's operating system.

Once inside the container, you can explore its file system, check running processes, or look at configuration files to help debug any issues.

Inspecting Container States with `docker inspect`

The `docker inspect` command gives you detailed information about a container, including network settings, configuration, volumes, and more. This can be useful if you're trying to troubleshoot an issue related to container configuration.

Example:

```
bash
```

```
docker inspect my-container
```

This will provide a JSON output with detailed information about the container. You can also filter the output to show only specific information using `--format`:

```
bash
```

```
docker inspect --format '{{.State.Running}}' my-
container
```

This will return `true` if the container is running or `false` if it is stopped.

Checking Resource Usage with `docker stats`

Docker also provides a command to monitor the real-time resource usage (CPU, memory, network) of running containers. This can be useful if you notice a container is consuming too many resources.

To monitor resource usage for all containers, use:

```
bash
```

```
docker stats
```

You can also monitor a specific container:

```
bash
```

```
docker stats my-container
```

This will display real-time statistics, helping you understand if the container is experiencing performance issues.

Summary:

In this chapter, we explored how to manage Docker containers by starting, stopping, and restarting them. We also discussed important container lifecycle management commands such as pausing, unpausing, and removing containers. Additionally, we covered how to debug container issues by using commands like `docker logs`, `docker exec`, and `docker inspect`, along with real-time monitoring of container resource usage. These skills are crucial for managing containers effectively and ensuring that your applications run smoothly.

CHAPTER 6

DOCKER NETWORKING: CONNECTING CONTAINERS

Overview of Docker Networking Modes (Bridge, Host, Overlay, etc.)

Docker provides several networking modes to connect containers to each other and the external network. Understanding these different modes is essential for choosing the right network configuration based on your use case.

1. Bridge Network

- **Default Network**: The **bridge network** is the default network mode when you create a container in Docker. When you run a container with no specific network configuration, it will be connected to the default bridge network.

- **How It Works**: Containers on the bridge network can communicate with each other using IP addresses, but they are isolated from the host system and external networks unless ports are explicitly exposed. A virtual Ethernet bridge is created on the host machine, and containers are

57

attached to this bridge. By default, containers on a bridge network can only communicate with each other if they know each other's IP address.

- **Use Case**: This network mode is useful when you want containers to be isolated from the host but still able to communicate with each other.

2. Host Network

- **How It Works**: When a container is run in **host mode**, it shares the host's network namespace. This means the container uses the host machine's IP address and network interfaces, effectively making the container part of the host's network.

- **Performance**: This mode offers improved network performance, as the container is directly connected to the host's network without the overhead of network address translation (NAT). It's ideal for high-performance applications that require low latency.

- **Use Case**: Host mode is typically used for performance-sensitive applications that need direct access to the host's networking stack (e.g., web servers, databases).

3. Overlay Network

- **How It Works**: The **overlay network** is used in Docker Swarm mode for creating multi-host container networks.

It allows containers running on different Docker hosts to communicate securely. This is achieved through the use of a VXLAN (Virtual Extensible LAN) tunnel that encapsulates network traffic.

- **Use Case**: Overlay networks are particularly useful for orchestrated environments like **Docker Swarm** or **Kubernetes**, where containers span multiple physical or virtual machines but still need to communicate with each other as if they are on the same local network.

4. None Network

- **How It Works**: Containers using the **none network** are completely isolated from the host machine and other containers. They do not have a network interface, and no external communication is possible unless specifically configured.
- **Use Case**: This mode is useful for running containers that do not require network access, such as batch jobs or applications that don't need to communicate with other systems.

5. Custom Networks

- **How It Works**: Docker allows you to create custom networks with specific configurations, such as specifying whether containers should use a bridge, host, or overlay network. This flexibility enables you to fine-tune network behavior for complex environments.

- **Use Case**: Custom networks are useful when you need granular control over container communication, especially when different services need isolated or specialized network configurations.

Setting Up a Container Network

To configure Docker networking, you can create a custom network and attach containers to it. Docker provides the `docker network` command to manage networks.

1. Creating a Custom Network

To create a custom network, you can use the following command:

```bash

docker network create --driver bridge my-network
```

This command creates a new **bridge** network named `my-network`. You can also specify other drivers like `host` or `overlay` if needed. By default, the `bridge` driver is used.

60

2. Running Containers on a Custom Network

Once the network is created, you can start containers on that network using the `--network` flag.

```bash
```

```
docker run -d --name my-container --network my-network nginx
```

This starts a container from the `nginx` image and attaches it to the `my-network` network. If no custom network is specified, the container would use the default bridge network.

3. Viewing Networks

To view the existing networks on your system, you can use the following command:

```bash
```

```
docker network ls
```

This will list all available networks, including the default ones (`bridge`, `host`, and `none`) and any custom networks you have created.

4. Inspecting a Network

To see detailed information about a specific network, use the `docker network inspect` command:

```bash
```

```
docker network inspect my-network
```

This will show detailed information about the network, including the containers attached to it and the network configuration.

Communicating Between Containers

One of the primary purposes of Docker networking is enabling containers to communicate with each other. By default, containers on the same custom network can communicate with each other by their container name or IP address.

1. Using Container Names to Communicate

When containers are on the same custom network, you can use their container names to establish communication. For example, if you have a container running a database and another container running a web application, the web container can communicate with the database container by using the database container's name.

Example:

- Start a database container:

```bash

docker run -d --name db-container --network
my-network mysql
```

- Start a web application container:

```bash

docker run -d --name web-container --
network my-network nginx
```

The web container can now access the database container by using db-container as the hostname. This is possible because both containers are attached to the same network (my-network).

2. Using the docker exec Command to Test Communication

To test communication between containers, you can use the docker exec command to execute commands inside a running container. For example, to test if the web container can connect to the database, you can run a ping command from the web container:

```bash
```

```
docker exec -it web-container ping db-container
```

If the ping is successful, it means the containers can communicate with each other over the network.

Exposing Ports and Configuring Firewall Rules

In Docker, exposing ports allows containers to communicate with external systems (including the host machine and other containers) through specified ports.

1. Exposing Ports to the Host System

By default, containers are isolated from the external network, but you can expose ports to allow communication with the host or external services. You do this using the -p option when running a container.

Example:

```
bash
```

```
docker run -d -p 8080:80 --name web-container
nginx
```

In this example, port 80 inside the container is mapped to port 8080 on the host. Now, you can access the web application running in the container by visiting `http://localhost:8080` in your web browser.

2. Exposing Ports to Other Containers

Containers can communicate with each other on a network without the need to expose ports to the host. However, if you want to expose ports between containers, you can do so using the `--expose` flag.

Example:

```bash
docker run -d --name my-container --expose 8080 my-image
```

This exposes port 8080 within the container to other containers on the same network.

3. Configuring Firewall Rules

When you expose a port, Docker automatically configures firewall rules to allow traffic to the container. You can also manually configure firewall settings on the host machine to control access to specific ports.

To ensure that only trusted sources can access the exposed port, you can use the `--publish` flag with specific IP addresses or IP ranges to restrict access. For example, to bind the exposed port to a specific interface:

```bash
docker run -d -p 192.168.1.100:8080:80 nginx
```

This binds port 8080 to IP `192.168.1.100` on the host, restricting access to that interface.

Summary:

In this chapter, we explored Docker networking modes, including **bridge**, **host**, **overlay**, and **none**, each offering different network isolation levels. We learned how to create custom networks and run containers on these networks, allowing for container-to-container communication. We also covered how to expose ports, both to the host system and to other containers, ensuring that applications inside containers can interact with the outside world. Finally, we discussed how to configure firewall rules to control access to containers based on exposed ports. Understanding these networking concepts is crucial for effectively connecting containers in a multi-container application or distributed environment.

CHAPTER 7

VOLUMES AND DATA PERSISTENCE

What Are Docker Volumes and Why They Are Essential?

In Docker, **volumes** are a key feature that allows you to manage persistent data in containers. Containers are typically ephemeral, meaning they are created, used, and destroyed, and any data stored inside them is lost when they are removed. To avoid losing important data when containers are stopped or removed, Docker provides volumes as a way to persist data outside the container's lifecycle.

Key Characteristics of Docker Volumes:

- **Persistent Storage**: Volumes are designed to persist data even when containers are stopped or removed. Unlike data stored inside the container's filesystem, data in volumes remains intact across container restarts and removals.
- **Shared Across Containers**: Volumes can be shared between multiple containers, which is particularly useful

when you need containers to share data, such as a database and a web server.

- **Managed by Docker**: Docker handles the lifecycle of volumes. You don't need to manage file system details; Docker abstracts that complexity.

- **Easier Backups and Migration**: Volumes are stored in a specific directory on the host, making them easy to back up or move between hosts, which is essential for managing production applications.

Managing Persistent Data in Docker Containers

While containers themselves are transient, you often need to retain certain data for purposes such as application state, configuration, or databases. Docker volumes provide a mechanism for handling this persistent data outside the ephemeral container environment.

Why Volumes Are Better Than Storing Data Inside Containers:

1. **Data Safety**: Data stored inside containers is lost when the container is deleted. By using volumes, you ensure that your data survives container recreation.

2. **Isolation**: Volumes are managed independently of the container, which allows you to easily move or backup data without affecting the container.

68

3. **Performance**: Docker volumes are optimized for performance. They use host filesystem features like the native file system for storage, ensuring efficient data handling.

Example of Using Volumes for Persistent Data:

- **Database**: If you're running a database inside a container, you would store the database files in a volume. This ensures that even if the database container is deleted, the data remains accessible when a new container is created.

Example:

bash

```
docker run -d --name mydb -v db-
data:/var/lib/mysql mysql
```

Here, db-data is the volume that will persist MySQL data outside the container.

Mounting Volumes for Data Persistence

To mount a volume to a Docker container, use the -v flag when running the container. The general syntax is:

bash

```
docker          run          -d          -v
<volume_name_or_path>:<container_path>
<image_name>
```

Types of Mounts:

1. **Named Volumes**: Docker can create and manage volumes by name. These volumes are stored in a default location managed by Docker (usually under `/var/lib/docker/volumes/`).

   Example:

   ```
   bash
   ```

   ```
   docker run -d -v my-volume:/data nginx
   ```

   In this example, Docker will automatically create the volume `my-volume` if it doesn't already exist. The volume will be mounted to the `/data` directory inside the container.

2. **Anonymous Volumes**: If you don't specify a name for the volume, Docker creates an anonymous volume that persists data. While this volume will survive container restarts, it's harder to track and manage since it's unnamed.

Example:

```bash
```

```
docker run -d -v /data nginx
```

Docker will create an anonymous volume and mount it to /data inside the container. You can see these volumes with docker volume ls, but they won't have an easily identifiable name.

Volume Mounts with Data Persistence:

- Volumes are persistent even if you stop, restart, or remove the container. As long as the volume exists, the data is preserved.
- For example, if you run a container that writes data to /data inside the container, the data will be stored in a volume and can be shared by other containers.

Viewing and Inspecting Volumes:

To view all volumes on your system:

```bash
```

```
docker volume ls
```

To inspect a specific volume and view its details:

71

```
bash
```

```
docker volume inspect my-volume
```

This command will show the volume's details, such as its location on the host filesystem.

Using Bind Mounts and Volume Drivers

While Docker volumes are designed for simplicity and portability, you may want to use **bind mounts** and **volume drivers** for more advanced use cases.

1. Bind Mounts

A **bind mount** allows you to mount a file or directory from the host system directly into the container. Unlike volumes, bind mounts link directly to a specific location on the host filesystem. This gives you more control but also requires you to manage the file paths.

How Bind Mounts Work:

- Bind mounts can point to any directory or file on the host system.
- Changes made to the mounted data are reflected on both the host and the container.

Example of mounting a host directory as a bind mount:

```
bash
```

```
docker          run          -d          -v
/path/on/host:/path/in/container nginx
```

In this example, `/path/on/host` is a directory on your host machine that is mounted to `/path/in/container` inside the container. Any changes made to the files inside `/path/in/container` will be reflected in `/path/on/host`.

Use Cases for Bind Mounts:

- **Development Environments**: Bind mounts are useful when you need to sync changes between your development environment on the host and the running container. For example, mounting your source code directory into a container so that code changes are immediately available in the container.
- **Config Files**: Mounting configuration files from the host system into a container.

2. Volume Drivers

While Docker provides default local storage for volumes, **volume drivers** allow you to extend Docker's capabilities for handling data storage. A volume driver allows you to use external storage

73

solutions like network-attached storage (NAS), cloud storage, or other external file systems.

Using Volume Drivers:

Docker has built-in drivers for managing volumes (like the `local` driver for local storage), but you can use third-party drivers to integrate Docker with other storage backends.

To create a volume with a specific driver:

```bash

docker volume create --driver <driver_name> my-volume
```

Example using an external volume driver (e.g., AWS EFS driver):

```bash

docker volume create --driver efs --name my-efs-volume
```

Volume drivers are especially useful in orchestrated environments like **Docker Swarm** or **Kubernetes**, where you may need to share volumes across multiple nodes in a distributed system.

Summary:

In this chapter, we explored how Docker handles data persistence through the use of volumes. We discussed how volumes are essential for managing persistent data outside of the container's lifecycle, which ensures that data is retained across container restarts or deletions. We also covered different methods for mounting volumes, including **named volumes**, **anonymous volumes**, and **bind mounts**, with examples of each. Finally, we introduced **volume drivers**, which extend Docker's ability to manage storage and integrate with external storage systems. Understanding these concepts will help you manage data effectively in your containerized applications, ensuring that critical data persists even as containers are created and destroyed.

CHAPTER 8

DOCKERFILE: AUTOMATING IMAGE CREATION

Introduction to Dockerfile and Its Syntax

A **Dockerfile** is a simple text file that contains a series of instructions that Docker uses to build an image. Each instruction in the Dockerfile creates a layer in the image, which Docker uses to efficiently build and manage images. The Dockerfile defines the environment in which your application will run, including which base image to use, which files to include, and how to configure the system inside the container.

Key Dockerfile Instructions:

- **FROM**: Specifies the base image to use for the Docker image. Every Dockerfile must start with a FROM statement.
- **RUN**: Executes a command in the container during the image build process, such as installing dependencies or setting up the environment.
- : Copies files from the host machine into the image.

- **ADD**: Similar to , but with additional functionality, like extracting tar archives or downloading files from URLs.
- **WORKDIR**: Sets the working directory for subsequent commands.
- **CMD**: Specifies the default command to run when the container starts.
- **EXPOSE**: Exposes a port so that it can be accessed from outside the container.
- **ENV**: Sets environment variables in the container.

Basic Syntax Example:

Here's a simple example of a Dockerfile that installs a Python application:

Dockerfile

```
# Use an official Python runtime as a base image
FROM python:3.9-slim

# Set the working directory in the container
WORKDIR /app

# the current directory contents into the container
. /app

# Install dependencies
RUN pip install -r requirements.txt
```

77

```
# Expose the port the app will run on
EXPOSE 8080

# Run the application
CMD ["python", "app.py"]
```

How to Write Your First Dockerfile

Writing your first Dockerfile is a straightforward process. Let's go step-by-step through creating a basic Dockerfile for a web application.

Step 1: Choose a Base Image

The first step is to choose a base image that matches the programming language or framework you're using. For example, if you're building a Python application, you might use the official Python image.

```
Dockerfile
```

```
FROM python:3.9-slim
```

Step 2: Set the Working Directory

The WORKDIR instruction sets the working directory inside the container. If the directory doesn't exist, it will be created automatically. This is where you will your project files.

```
Dockerfile
```

```
WORKDIR /app
```

Step 3: Files

Use the command to files from your local machine to the container. For example, to your entire application into the /app directory in the container:

```
Dockerfile
```

```
. /app
```

Step 4: Install Dependencies

If your project has dependencies (for example, a requirements.txt file for Python), you can install them using the RUN command.

```
Dockerfile
```

```
RUN pip install -r requirements.txt
```

Step 5: Expose a Port

If your application listens on a specific port, you can expose that port using the EXPOSE instruction. This allows you to map the container port to a host port when running the container.

```
Dockerfile
```

79

```
EXPOSE 8080
```

Step 6: Set the Default Command

The CMD instruction specifies the default command to run when the container starts. In this case, we're running a Python application.

Dockerfile

```
CMD ["python", "app.py"]
```

Complete Dockerfile Example:

Here's the complete Dockerfile for a basic Python application:

Dockerfile

```
# Use an official Python runtime as a base image
FROM python:3.9-slim

# Set the working directory in the container
WORKDIR /app

#   the   current   directory   contents   into   the
container
 . /app

# Install dependencies
RUN pip install -r requirements.txt
```

```
# Expose the port the app will run on
EXPOSE 8080

# Run the application
CMD ["python", "app.py"]
```

To build the image from this Dockerfile, run the following command in the directory containing the Dockerfile:

```bash
```

```
docker build -t my-python-app .
```

This will create an image named `my-python-app`, and you can run it using:

```bash
```

```
docker run -p 8080:8080 my-python-app
```

Optimizing Dockerfiles for Smaller and Faster Builds

While writing Dockerfiles, it's important to optimize them for **smaller image sizes** and **faster build times**. Here are some best practices for achieving that:

81

1. Use Official and Minimal Base Images

Choose official base images that are optimized for minimal size. For example, `python:3.9-slim` is a smaller version of the `python:3.9` image, containing only the essential libraries required to run Python.

Avoid using large base images with unnecessary tools and libraries unless absolutely necessary.

2. Combine RUN Commands

Every `RUN` instruction creates a new layer in the image. To reduce the number of layers and the size of the image, combine multiple `RUN` commands into a single instruction.

Instead of:

```Dockerfile
RUN apt-get update
RUN apt-get install -y curl
```

Use:

```Dockerfile
RUN apt-get update && apt-get install -y curl
```

This reduces the number of layers and speeds up the build process.

3. Clean Up After Installing Dependencies

When installing dependencies, make sure to clean up unnecessary files to keep the image size small. For example, you can remove package manager cache files after installing packages:

```
Dockerfile
```

```
RUN apt-get update && apt-get install -y curl &&
rm -rf /var/lib/apt/lists/*
```

4. Leverage Docker Build Cache

Docker caches intermediate layers during the build process. To take advantage of this, you should order your Dockerfile so that instructions that change less frequently (e.g., installing dependencies) are placed before instructions that change more frequently (e.g., ing application files). This minimizes the need to rebuild layers unnecessarily.

For example:

```
Dockerfile
```

```
 requirements.txt /app/
RUN pip install -r requirements.txt
 . /app/
```

In this example, Docker will only rebuild the layers involving the and `RUN` commands if `requirements.txt` changes. If only application files change, Docker will reuse the cached layers.

Multi-Stage Builds in Docker

Multi-stage builds allow you to create Docker images in multiple stages, which can help reduce the size of the final image by excluding unnecessary build artifacts.

What Are Multi-Stage Builds?

A multi-stage build allows you to use one image for compiling and building your application and a second, lighter image for running it. This is particularly useful for languages like Go, Java, and Python, where dependencies and build tools are required during the build but are not needed in the final container.

Example of Multi-Stage Build:

Let's say you are building a Go application. During the build, you need Go's development tools, but you don't want to include them in the final image. With a multi-stage build, you can separate these concerns.

```
Dockerfile
```

84

```
# First stage: build the Go app
FROM golang:1.16 AS builder
WORKDIR /app

  .  .

RUN go build -o my-app .

# Second stage: create a smaller image with the
Go binary
FROM alpine:latest
WORKDIR /app
 --from=builder /app/my-app .
CMD ["./my-app"]
```

Explanation:

- The first stage (golang:1.16) compiles the Go application and creates a binary.
- The second stage uses a much smaller alpine:latest image and copies only the compiled binary from the first stage.

This results in a much smaller final image, as it contains only the application and its necessary runtime environment, without any development dependencies.

Summary:

In this chapter, we covered how to write a Dockerfile to automate the creation of Docker images. We explored the basic syntax of Dockerfiles, including key instructions such as FROM, RUN, , WORKDIR, EXPOSE, and CMD. We also discussed best practices for optimizing Dockerfiles, such as using minimal base images, combining RUN commands, cleaning up after installations, and leveraging Docker's build cache. Finally, we delved into **multi-stage builds**, which allow for more efficient and smaller images by separating the build and runtime environments. These practices will help you create clean, optimized Docker images that are smaller, faster to build, and easier to maintain.

CHAPTER 9

BUILDING AND CUSTOMIZING DOCKER IMAGES

The `docker build` Command Explained

The `docker build` command is used to create Docker images from a Dockerfile. This command reads the instructions in the Dockerfile, executes them in order, and produces an image that can be run as a container. The basic syntax for the `docker build` command is as follows:

```bash

docker        build        -t        <image_name>:<tag>
<path_to_dockerfile>
```

Key Components of the `docker build` Command:

- **-t <image_name>:<tag>**: This option tags the image with a name and version. If you don't specify a tag, it defaults to `latest`.

- **<path_to_dockerfile>**: This is the directory containing the Dockerfile and the context (files and directories) that will be used during the build. If your

87

Dockerfile is in the current directory, you can use . to specify the path.

Example:

```
bash
```

```
docker build -t my-python-app:1.0 .
```

This command will build a Docker image from the Dockerfile in the current directory and tag it as my-python-app:1.0.

Building Images from Dockerfiles

A **Dockerfile** defines how the Docker image will be built. It contains a series of instructions that specify the base image, dependencies, environment variables, and the commands to run in the container.

Basic Example of a Dockerfile:

Let's say you are building a Python application. Here is a simple Dockerfile for this case:

```
Dockerfile
```

```
# Use an official Python runtime as a base image
FROM python:3.9-slim
```

88

```
# Set the working directory in the container
WORKDIR /app

# the current directory contents into the
container
  . /app

# Install dependencies
RUN pip install -r requirements.txt

# Expose port for the application
EXPOSE 8080

# Define the command to run the application
CMD ["python", "app.py"]
```

Steps for Building the Image:

1. **Create the Dockerfile**: Save the Dockerfile in your project directory.

2. **Build the Image**: Run the `docker build` command to build the image from the Dockerfile:

   bash

   ```
   docker build -t my-python-app:1.0 .
   ```

3. **Verify the Image**: Once the build is complete, use the `docker images` command to verify the image is listed:

```
bash

docker images
```

This will display a list of all Docker images on your system, including my-python-app:1.0.

Image Versioning and Tagging

When building Docker images, it's essential to use **versioning and tagging** to organize and differentiate images. By default, Docker tags the image as latest if no specific tag is provided, but it's a best practice to version your images.

Tagging Images:

- **Tags** are used to identify different versions of an image. Tags follow the format <image_name>:<tag>, where <image_name> is the name of the image, and <tag> is a version number or label (e.g., 1.0, v2, stable).
- The **tag** helps you maintain multiple versions of the same image. For example, you might have my-python-app:1.0 for the first version of your app and my-python-app:2.0 for the second version.

Example of tagging an image:

bash

```
docker build -t my-python-app:1.0 .
```

To **retag an existing image**, use the `docker tag` command:

bash

```
docker tag my-python-app:1.0 my-python-app:v1
```

Now, you have two tags (`1.0` and `v1`) pointing to the same image.

Pushing Tagged Images to a Registry:

After building and tagging your image, you can push it to a registry like Docker Hub to share with others.

bash

```
docker push my-python-app:1.0
```

If you're pushing a custom image to Docker Hub, you'll need to use your Docker Hub username as part of the image name:

bash

```
docker tag my-python-app:1.0 username/my-python-app:1.0
docker push username/my-python-app:1.0
```

Docker Image Layers and Caching

One of the key features of Docker is its use of **image layers** and **caching**, which helps optimize build performance and reduce the size of images.

Image Layers Explained:

Each instruction in a Dockerfile creates a **new layer** in the resulting image. For example, the FROM instruction creates the first layer (the base image), and each RUN, , or ADD instruction creates a new layer on top of it. These layers are stacked on top of each other to form the final image.

- **Base Layer**: The FROM statement specifies the base image, which is the first layer of your image.
- **Intermediate Layers**: Each subsequent command in the Dockerfile (e.g., RUN, , ADD) adds a layer.
- **Final Image**: The top-most layer is the final image, which is what Docker runs when a container is started.

How Layer Caching Works:

Docker uses **build cache** to optimize builds. When Docker builds an image, it checks the instructions in the Dockerfile and reuses layers that haven't changed. If a layer has been built before and hasn't been modified, Docker uses the cached version instead of rebuilding it, which makes subsequent builds faster.

92

For example:

1. **First Build**: Docker runs every instruction in the Dockerfile and creates a new layer for each.
2. **Subsequent Builds**: If the Dockerfile hasn't changed, Docker will use the cached layers, making the build process faster.

However, if you modify an instruction that appears earlier in the Dockerfile, all subsequent layers must be rebuilt, even if the other instructions haven't changed.

Best Practices for Efficient Caching:

1. **Order Commands Smartly**: Place commands that are less likely to change (e.g., installing dependencies) towards the top of the Dockerfile. This way, Docker can reuse cached layers if the files don't change frequently.

   Example:

   ```
   Dockerfile
   ```

   ```
   requirements.txt /app/
   RUN pip install -r requirements.txt
    . /app/
   ```

   In this example, if `requirements.txt` changes, only the layers that depend on it will be rebuilt. But if other files change (e.g., application code), Docker will reuse the cached layers for installing dependencies.

2. **Minimize the Number of Layers**: Every instruction (e.g., RUN,) adds a layer to the image. Combine multiple instructions into a single RUN statement to reduce the number of layers.

Example:

```
Dockerfile
```

```
RUN apt-get update && apt-get install -y
curl && rm -rf /var/lib/apt/lists/*
```

This combines multiple commands into one RUN instruction, reducing the image size by having fewer layers.

Summary:

In this chapter, we explored the docker build command, which is used to build Docker images from a Dockerfile. We discussed how to write a Dockerfile and the syntax of common Dockerfile instructions like FROM, RUN, , and CMD. We also covered the importance of **image versioning and tagging** for managing multiple versions of your images, as well as how to push tagged images to a registry like Docker Hub.

We then examined **Docker image layers and caching**, which help optimize image builds and reduce redundancy. By understanding how Docker reuses layers and caches previous builds, you can make your image creation faster and more efficient. By following best practices for Dockerfile creation, such as ordering commands intelligently and minimizing the number of layers, you can ensure your Docker images are optimized for size and build speed.

CHAPTER 10

DOCKER COMPOSE: MULTI-CONTAINER APPLICATIONS

Introduction to Docker Compose

Docker Compose is a tool that allows you to define and manage multi-container Docker applications. It simplifies the process of configuring and running multiple containers that work together as part of a single application. Instead of manually running individual containers and managing networking, Docker Compose allows you to define your entire multi-container setup in a single configuration file and manage the containers as a group.

Docker Compose is ideal for applications that require multiple services, such as a web application with a database, cache, and messaging system, or microservices architectures where each service runs in its own container.

With Docker Compose, you define your application's services, networks, and volumes in a **docker-compose.yml** file. The file describes how the different containers should be built, connected, and configured. This makes it easier to manage and deploy applications that require more than one container.

Writing `docker-compose.yml` Files

The core component of Docker Compose is the **docker-compose.yml** file, which defines all the services that make up the application, along with their configurations and dependencies. The file is written in **YAML** format, which is human-readable and allows for easy configuration.

Basic Structure of `docker-compose.yml`:

A basic `docker-compose.yml` file might look like this:

yaml

```yaml
version: '3'
services:
  web:
    image: nginx:latest
    ports:
      - "8080:80"
    volumes:
      - ./html:/usr/share/nginx/html
  db:
    image: mysql:5.7
    environment:
      MYSQL_ROOT_PASSWORD: example
    volumes:
      - db-data:/var/lib/mysql
volumes:
```

```
db-data:
```

Let's break it down:

- **version**: Specifies the version of the Docker Compose file format (in this case, version 3).
- **services**: Lists all the containers (services) that make up the application. Each service is defined with a set of properties.
  - o `web`: The name of the web service.
    - ▪ `image`: Specifies the Docker image to use for the container.
    - ▪ `ports`: Maps port 80 inside the container to port 8080 on the host.
    - ▪ `volumes`: Mounts a local directory (`./html`) to a directory inside the container (`/usr/share/nginx/html`).
  - o `db`: The name of the database service.
    - ▪ `image`: Specifies the MySQL image to use.
    - ▪ `environment`: Sets environment variables for the container, such as the MySQL root password.
    - ▪ `volumes`: Creates a named volume (`db-data`) for persistent storage.
- **volumes**: Defines named volumes that are used to store data persistently.

How Docker Compose Works:

- **Build and Run**: With a properly defined `docker-compose.yml` file, you can use `docker-compose` commands to build and manage the multi-container application.

  To start all services defined in the `docker-compose.yml` file:

  ```bash
  docker-compose up
  ```

  This will pull the required images (if they are not available locally), create containers for each service, and start them.

  To stop the services:

  ```bash
  docker-compose down
  ```

Managing Multi-Container Apps with Compose

Docker Compose makes it easier to manage multi-container applications by automating container orchestration, networking, and volumes. Here's how Docker Compose handles these tasks:

1. Managing Networking:

Docker Compose automatically creates a network for your containers. All services defined in the `docker-compose.yml` file are connected to this network by default, allowing them to communicate with each other using their service names.

For example, in the `docker-compose.yml` file from earlier, the `web` container can connect to the `db` container using the service name `db` (e.g., `db:3306`), instead of using IP addresses or ports.

2. Managing Volumes:

Docker Compose can automatically manage shared volumes between containers. For example, the database container's data is persisted using the `db-data` volume, which is defined in the `docker-compose.yml` file and shared between multiple containers if needed.

3. Managing Dependencies:

Docker Compose allows you to define dependencies between containers using the depends_on option. This ensures that one container starts before another, which is useful when you have services that depend on the availability of others.

For example, you could define a dependency where the web service depends on the db service:

yaml

```
services:
  web:
    image: nginx:latest
    depends_on:
      - db
  db:
    image: mysql:5.7
```

Docker Compose will start the db service first and ensure it is running before starting the web service.

4. Scaling Services:

With Docker Compose, you can easily scale services to run multiple instances of a container. This is particularly useful for applications that require high availability.

For example, to scale the web service to 3 instances, use the following command:

```bash
```

```
docker-compose up --scale web=3
```

This will start three web containers, each running behind the same load balancer (if you've set up a reverse proxy like Nginx).

Practical Examples of Using Docker Compose for Microservices

Microservices architecture often involves multiple services working together as a single application. Docker Compose is ideal for orchestrating the various components in a microservices application. Let's look at a practical example of using Docker Compose for a simple microservices-based app.

Example 1: A Web Application with a Database and a Cache

In this example, we have three services:

1. **Web**: A web application (e.g., an API or a front-end server).
2. **Database**: A MySQL database.
3. **Cache**: A Redis cache.

102

Here's how you might set up the `docker-compose.yml` file:

```yaml
version: '3'

services:
  web:
    image: my-web-app
    build: ./web
    depends_on:
      - db
      - cache
    environment:
      - DB_HOST=db
      - CACHE_HOST=cache
    ports:
      - "5000:5000"

  db:
    image: mysql:5.7
    environment:
      MYSQL_ROOT_PASSWORD: mypassword
    volumes:
      - db-data:/var/lib/mysql

  cache:
    image: redis:alpine
    volumes:
      - cache-data:/data
```

```
volumes:
  db-data:
  cache-data:
```

Explanation:

- **Web Service**: This service is the web application, which builds from a local Dockerfile (`./web`). It depends on both the `db` and `cache` services, ensuring they are started first.

- **Database Service**: This service runs a MySQL container, and the `MYSQL_ROOT_PASSWORD` is set via environment variables. The database data is persisted using a named volume (`db-data`).

- **Cache Service**: This service runs a Redis container, using a named volume (`cache-data`) to persist cache data.

Scaling the Web Application:

To scale the web application to multiple instances, run:

```bash
bash
```

```
docker-compose up --scale web=3
```

This will spin up three instances of the `web` service, which can be load balanced behind a reverse proxy like Nginx.

Example 2: Microservices with API Gateway

A more complex example of a microservices application using Docker Compose includes an **API Gateway** in front of multiple microservices. This architecture often uses Nginx or another reverse proxy to route requests to different services based on the URL or path.

yaml

```
version: '3'

services:
  api-gateway:
    image: nginx:latest
    volumes:
      - ./nginx.conf:/etc/nginx/nginx.conf
    ports:
      - "80:80"

  service1:
    image: my-service1
    build: ./service1
    expose:
      - "3000"

  service2:
    image: my-service2
```

105

```
build: ./service2
expose:
  - "4000"
```

In this setup:

- The `api-gateway` service uses Nginx to route incoming traffic to either `service1` or `service2`.
- Both `service1` and `service2` expose internal ports (3000 and 4000, respectively) without mapping them to the host machine, as they will be accessed via the gateway.

Summary:

In this chapter, we explored Docker Compose, a powerful tool for managing multi-container applications. We covered how to write a `docker-compose.yml` file to define services, networks, and volumes. We also discussed how Docker Compose manages networking, scaling, and dependencies between containers. Finally, we looked at practical examples of using Docker Compose for microservices, including a simple web application with a database and a cache, as well as a more advanced example with an API gateway. Docker Compose makes it easy to orchestrate and manage complex applications that consist of multiple containers, simplifying deployment and scaling.

CHAPTER 11

WORKING WITH DOCKER REGISTRIES

Docker Hub vs. Private Registries

A **Docker registry** is a place where Docker images are stored and shared. Docker uses registries to store and distribute images that you can pull and use in your containers. There are two main types of registries: **Docker Hub** (public) and **private registries** (self-hosted or third-party services).

1. Docker Hub

- **Public Registry**: Docker Hub is the default and most widely used Docker registry. It's publicly accessible, meaning anyone can pull images from it. It's home to thousands of popular images, including official images for programming languages, databases, web servers, and more.

- **Free and Paid Tiers**: Docker Hub offers both free and paid plans. The free plan allows you to pull and push public images, while the paid plan provides private

107

repositories for storing images that are not publicly available.

- **Official Images**: Docker Hub hosts a collection of official images maintained by the Docker team or trusted third parties, which are optimized, secure, and frequently updated.

2. Private Registries

- **Self-Hosted Registries**: If you want more control over your images, especially for sensitive or proprietary data, you can set up a private Docker registry. This can be hosted on your own infrastructure or in the cloud.
- **Third-Party Registries**: Many cloud service providers, such as **Amazon Elastic Container Registry (ECR)**, **Google Container Registry (GCR)**, and **Azure Container Registry (ACR)**, offer private registry services as part of their platform.
- **Security**: Private registries offer more security features, including access control and encryption. You can configure who has access to your images and restrict the pulling and pushing of images to only authorized users.

Choosing between Docker Hub and a private registry depends on the following factors:

- **Public vs. Private Images**: If your images need to be public, Docker Hub is a great choice. If they need to remain private, you should use a private registry.
- **Control and Security**: For more control and enhanced security (e.g., enterprise-grade access control), a private registry is the preferred option.

Pushing and Pulling Images to and from Docker Hub

Docker Hub is widely used for sharing images between developers, teams, and the community. You can push your images to Docker Hub, and pull images from it to use in your containers.

1. Pushing Images to Docker Hub

To push an image to Docker Hub, you need to follow these steps:

- **Step 1: Log in to Docker Hub**

    Before pushing an image, ensure you're logged into Docker Hub using the `docker login` command. This will authenticate your Docker client with Docker Hub.

    bash

    ```
    docker login
    ```

You will be prompted for your Docker Hub username and password. Once authenticated, you can proceed to push images.

- **Step 2: Tag the Image**

Docker images need to be tagged with the correct repository name and tag before pushing. The tag follows the format: `<username>/<repository>:<tag>`. For example, to tag an image as `username/my-app:latest`, use the following command:

```bash
docker tag my-app username/my-app:latest
```

- **Step 3: Push the Image**

Once the image is tagged, you can push it to Docker Hub using the `docker push` command:

```bash
docker push username/my-app:latest
```

Docker will upload the image to Docker Hub, and it will be available under the specified repository.

2. Pulling Images from Docker Hub

To pull an image from Docker Hub, you use the `docker pull` command:

bash

```
docker pull username/my-app:latest
```

If you don't specify a tag, Docker defaults to pulling the `latest` tag.

You can also pull official images by their name:

bash

```
docker pull nginx
```

This will pull the latest `nginx` image from Docker Hub.

Setting Up and Managing a Private Registry

Setting up a private registry is useful for securely storing and managing your Docker images. Docker provides an easy-to-use registry solution, which you can deploy and host on your infrastructure.

1. Setting Up a Private Docker Registry

To set up a private Docker registry, Docker provides an official registry image that you can run as a container.

- **Step 1: Pull the Docker Registry Image**

  First, you need to pull the official Docker registry image:

  ```bash
  docker pull registry
  ```

- **Step 2: Run the Registry Container**

  Next, run the Docker registry container. By default, the registry will listen on port 5000.

  ```bash
  docker run -d -p 5000:5000 --name registry registry:2
  ```

  This command runs the registry container in detached mode (-d) and maps port 5000 on your host to port 5000 on the container.

- **Step 3: Pushing Images to Your Private Registry**

Once the registry is running, you can push images to it just like you would with Docker Hub. First, tag the image with your private registry's address (e.g., `localhost:5000`):

bash

```
docker tag my-app localhost:5000/my-app
```

Then push the image to your private registry:

bash

```
docker push localhost:5000/my-app
```

- **Step 4: Pulling Images from Your Private Registry**

To pull the image back from the private registry, you use the following command:

bash

```
docker pull localhost:5000/my-app
```

2. Configuring Authentication and Security for Private Registries

To secure your private registry, you can enable basic authentication, use SSL/TLS encryption, and configure access control lists (ACLs) to limit access to specific users.

113

- **SSL/TLS**: For secure communication, it's recommended to run your private registry over HTTPS. You can configure SSL certificates by following Docker's official SSL guide.

- **Authentication**: You can set up basic authentication to require users to log in before pushing or pulling images. Docker allows you to integrate with third-party authentication providers or use HTTP basic authentication with passwords.

- **Access Control**: Docker Registry supports access control lists (ACLs), which allow you to define user roles and permissions for pushing and pulling images.

Best Practices for Managing Images in a Registry

Managing Docker images in a registry involves more than just pushing and pulling. Here are some best practices to keep your images organized and secure:

1. Use Descriptive Image Tags

Always use **descriptive tags** to differentiate between various versions of your images. For example:

- Use version numbers (1.0, 1.1, 2.0).

- Use descriptive tags like `latest`, `stable`, or `dev` to indicate the purpose of the image.

Example:

```bash

docker tag my-app:1.0 username/my-app:v1.0
```

2. Clean Up Unused Images

Over time, your registry can become cluttered with unused or outdated images. To keep things clean, regularly delete images that are no longer needed. In Docker Hub, you can delete images from the web interface, while in a private registry, you can use the `docker registry garbage-collect` command to remove unreferenced layers.

3. Use Automated Builds

If you have a continuous integration/continuous deployment (CI/CD) pipeline, automate the building and pushing of Docker images. Docker Hub offers automated builds, or you can use third-party CI/CD tools like Jenkins, GitLab CI, or CircleCI to automatically build and push images whenever your code changes.

4. Monitor Registry Usage

If you're using a private registry, monitor its usage to ensure it has enough resources for storing and serving images. This can include monitoring disk usage, number of images, and the frequency of image pulls and pushes.

5. Security and Access Control

Ensure your registry is secure by using encryption (SSL/TLS), authentication (via Docker's login system or third-party solutions), and proper access control. Define user roles and permissions to limit who can push, pull, or delete images.

Summary:

In this chapter, we explored how to work with Docker registries, starting with the difference between **Docker Hub** (public) and **private registries**. We discussed how to push and pull images to and from Docker Hub and the process of setting up and managing a private registry using Docker's official registry image. Finally, we covered best practices for managing Docker images in a registry, including using descriptive tags, cleaning up unused images, automating builds, and securing the registry. By following these practices, you can efficiently manage and share

Docker images within your organization or the broader community.

CHAPTER 12

DOCKER FOR DEVELOPMENT WORKFLOWS

Docker in a Local Development Environment

Docker is increasingly being used in local development environments because it provides a consistent, isolated, and reproducible environment for developing, testing, and debugging applications. Docker makes it easy to set up development environments that are isolated from the host system, ensuring that dependencies, configurations, and operating systems are consistent across all developers' machines.

Benefits of Using Docker in Local Development:

1. **Environment Consistency**: By using Docker, developers can ensure that all team members are working with the same environment. This avoids "works on my machine" issues where applications behave differently on different developers' machines due to differing configurations, libraries, or operating systems.

2. **Quick Setup and Tear Down**: With Docker, setting up and tearing down environments is simple. You can

quickly spin up containers for databases, web servers, or other services, and shut them down once you're done with them, without affecting the host machine.

3. **Isolation**: Docker containers provide a clean, isolated environment for each application, so dependencies and libraries for one project won't interfere with another. This is particularly useful when working on multiple projects with different dependencies.

4. **Reproducibility**: Docker allows you to define your development environment in a `Dockerfile`, which makes it easy to replicate the environment on different machines. It ensures that the environment you develop in is the same as the one you deploy to production.

Setting Up a Local Development Environment with Docker:

1. **Creating a Dockerfile for Your Development Environment**: The first step in using Docker for local development is creating a `Dockerfile` that sets up your development environment. This may include the base image (e.g., `node`, `python`, `ruby`), the installation of dependencies, and any configuration steps needed for your app.

   Example Dockerfile for a Node.js development environment:

```
Dockerfile

FROM node:14

WORKDIR /app

 package.json /app/
RUN npm install

 . /app/

EXPOSE 3000
CMD ["npm", "start"]
```

2. **Building the Image**: Once you've created your `Dockerfile`, you can build the image using:

```bash
bash
```

```
docker build -t my-dev-env .
```

3. **Running the Container**: After building the image, you can run the container and bind it to a port on your local machine:

```bash
bash
```

```
docker run -d -p 3000:3000 --name dev-container my-dev-env
```

This command will run your development environment container in the background and map port 3000 inside the container to port 3000 on your local machine.

Using Docker for Testing and Continuous Integration

Docker is also commonly used in testing and continuous integration (CI) pipelines. The isolation provided by Docker containers allows for repeatable and predictable tests and builds in CI/CD workflows.

Benefits of Using Docker in Testing:

1. **Reproducible Test Environments**: By using Docker, you can ensure that your tests always run in the same environment, with the same dependencies, regardless of where the tests are executed (on local machines, CI servers, or production environments).

2. **Isolation of Tests**: Running tests in Docker containers ensures that they won't interfere with the host system or other tests. Each test can be run in its own isolated container, which helps prevent test contamination.

3. **Speed and Efficiency**: Docker allows you to quickly create and destroy containers for testing, making it much faster than setting up separate VMs for each test scenario.

Using Docker for CI/CD Pipelines:

In a CI pipeline, Docker is typically used to build, test, and deploy applications in a repeatable and isolated environment. Here's how Docker fits into the CI/CD process:

1. **Build Stage**: In the build stage, Docker can be used to create the application image by building from a `Dockerfile`. This ensures that the application is built consistently, no matter where the build takes place.

   Example CI configuration for building the Docker image:

   yaml

   ```
   version: '3'
   services:
     build:
       dockerfile: Dockerfile
       context: .
       image: my-app:latest
   ```

2. **Test Stage**: After building the image, the next step is running tests inside a container. For example, you can run your tests inside the container to ensure that the app behaves as expected.

   Example of running tests in a Docker container:

```bash
bash
```

```
docker run --rm my-app:latest npm test
```

3. **Deploy Stage**: Once the tests are successful, Docker can be used to deploy the image to production or a staging environment. This is usually done by pushing the image to a registry like Docker Hub or a private registry and then pulling and running it in the production environment.

Automating Development Workflows with Docker Compose

For applications with multiple services, such as microservices architectures or multi-component applications, **Docker Compose** allows you to automate the management of these services. Docker Compose allows you to define and manage multi-container applications with a single YAML file (`docker-compose.yml`).

Setting Up a Development Environment with Docker Compose:

Suppose you are developing a web application that requires a database and a caching service. With Docker Compose, you can define the services (e.g., web, db, cache) in one configuration file and manage them as a single unit.

Here's an example `docker-compose.yml` file for a simple web application with a Node.js backend, MySQL database, and Redis cache:

```yaml
version: '3'

services:
  web:
    image: my-node-app
    build: ./web
    ports:
      - "3000:3000"
    depends_on:
      - db
      - cache
    environment:
      - DB_HOST=db
      - CACHE_HOST=cache

  db:
    image: mysql:5.7
    environment:
      MYSQL_ROOT_PASSWORD: example
    volumes:
      - db-data:/var/lib/mysql

  cache:
```

```
image: redis:alpine
volumes:
  - cache-data:/data

volumes:
  db-data:
  cache-data:
```

Explanation:

- **web**: This service runs the Node.js web application and maps port 3000 to the host machine. It depends on the db and cache services, which means they will be started before the web service.
- **db**: This service runs a MySQL container with a root password, and its data is persisted using the db-data volume.
- **cache**: This service runs a Redis container with persistent cache data stored in the cache-data volume.

Running the Application with Docker Compose:

To start the services defined in the docker-compose.yml file, use:

```bash

docker-compose up
```

Docker Compose will automatically pull the necessary images, build the ones that need to be built, and start the containers in the correct order.

To stop the services and remove the containers, use:

bash

docker-compose down

Scaling Services:

You can also scale services using Docker Compose. For example, to run multiple instances of the web service, you can use:

bash

docker-compose up --scale web=3

This command will start three containers for the web service, load balancing requests across them.

Managing Environment Variables in Containers

In Docker, **environment variables** are used to pass configuration data to containers. Environment variables are especially useful for configuring settings that might change between different

126

environments (development, staging, production), such as database credentials, API keys, or app configuration.

Setting Environment Variables:

You can set environment variables for containers in several ways:

1. **In the Dockerfile**: You can use the ENV instruction in the Dockerfile to set environment variables that will be available to all containers created from the image.

```
Dockerfile

ENV DB_HOST=db
ENV CACHE_HOST=cache
```

2. **In the docker-compose.yml File**: You can define environment variables in the docker-compose.yml file under the environment key.

```
yaml

version: '3'

services:
  web:
    image: my-node-app
    environment:
```

```
    - DB_HOST=db
    - CACHE_HOST=cache
```

3. **Using an .env File**:
   Docker Compose supports environment variable
   substitution using an .env file. You can define variables
   in the .env file and reference them in your docker-
   compose.yml.

   Example .env file:

```
ini
```

```
DB_HOST=db
CACHE_HOST=cache
```

   In docker-compose.yml:

```
yaml
```

```
version: '3'

services:
  web:
    image: my-node-app
    environment:
      - DB_HOST=${DB_HOST}
      - CACHE_HOST=${CACHE_HOST}
```

Accessing Environment Variables Inside Containers:

You can access the environment variables inside the container in the same way you would access them on a normal operating system, depending on the language and framework you're using. For example, in Node.js, you would use:

```javascript
const dbHost = process.env.DB_HOST;
const cacheHost = process.env.CACHE_HOST;
```

Summary:

In this chapter, we discussed how Docker can be used to improve development workflows. We explored how Docker helps ensure consistent environments, making development, testing, and deployment faster and more predictable. We also covered how to use Docker Compose for managing multi-container applications, including setting up development environments with multiple services like a web server, database, and cache. Finally, we examined how to manage environment variables in Docker containers, enabling configuration flexibility and making it easier to work across different environments (development, staging, production). With Docker, developers can automate and streamline their workflows, ensuring that the environment in which they develop is consistent and reproducible.

CHAPTER 13

DEBUGGING AND TROUBLESHOOTING DOCKER CONTAINERS

Using `docker logs`, `docker exec`, *and* `docker inspect` *for Troubleshooting*

Docker provides several tools to help you troubleshoot and debug containers when things go wrong. These tools help you view container logs, interact with running containers, and inspect the container's configuration and state.

1. Using `docker logs` for Troubleshooting

The `docker logs` command retrieves the logs of a running or stopped container. This is useful for checking the output of the application running inside the container, especially when you need to debug issues related to the container's operation.

To view the logs of a specific container:

bash

```
docker logs <container_name_or_id>
```

You can use various options to refine the log output:

- **-f**: Follow the logs in real-time, similar to `tail -f`.

  Example:

  ```bash
  docker logs -f my-container
  ```

- **--tail**: Show only the last N lines of logs.

  Example:

  ```bash
  docker logs --tail 100 my-container
  ```

- **--since** / **--until**: Show logs since or until a specific time.

  Example:

  ```bash
  docker logs --since "2025-04-01T00:00:00" my-container
  ```

2. Using `docker exec` for Interactive Debugging

The `docker exec` command allows you to execute commands inside a running container, making it a powerful tool for debugging. You can use `docker exec` to inspect the container's filesystem, run shell commands, or interact with the application running inside the container.

To start an interactive shell session inside a container:

```bash
docker exec -it <container_name_or_id> /bin/bash
```

This will give you access to a shell inside the container, allowing you to navigate the filesystem, check logs, or run debugging commands directly inside the container.

Example:

```bash
docker exec -it my-container /bin/bash
```

Once inside the container, you can use standard Linux commands to investigate issues, such as checking log files or running diagnostic commands (`ps`, `top`, `df`, etc.).

3. Using `docker inspect` for Deep Container Insights

The `docker inspect` command provides detailed information about a container's configuration, including network settings, environment variables, volumes, and more. This is useful when you need to see how a container was configured or to troubleshoot specific issues related to networking or storage.

To inspect a container:

bash

```
docker inspect <container_name_or_id>
```

This will return a detailed JSON output with information about the container's state, including:

- Network settings
- Mounted volumes
- Environment variables
- Configurations and command-line arguments

You can use the `--format` option to extract specific information from the output. For example, to view the container's IP address:

bash

```
docker inspect --format '{{.NetworkSettings.IPAddress}}' my-container
```

133

Common Issues and Fixes in Docker Containers

While Docker simplifies containerized application management, you may encounter several common issues when running containers. Here are some of the most frequently encountered issues and how to resolve them:

1. Container Crashes or Stops Unexpectedly

- **Cause**: The container's entry point or command (`CMD` in the Dockerfile) may have failed, or the application inside the container crashed.
- **Solution**: Use `docker logs` to check the container logs and look for any errors related to the application's startup. Check the error message or stack trace to determine the root cause. Often, misconfigured environment variables or missing dependencies are the culprits.

Example:

```bash
docker logs my-container
```

2. Port Binding Issues

- **Cause**: The container may not be able to bind to the desired port on the host machine, either because the port is already in use or because the container isn't exposing the correct port.

- **Solution**: Ensure the port you want to bind to is not already being used by another application or container. You can use `docker ps` to view all running containers and their port bindings. If the container is not exposing the port, check the Dockerfile to ensure the `EXPOSE` instruction is set correctly.

Example:

```bash
```

```
docker ps
```

3. Network Connectivity Problems Between Containers

- **Cause**: Containers on different networks or with misconfigured networking settings may not be able to communicate with each other.

- **Solution**: Use `docker network ls` to list available networks and ensure that the containers are on the correct network. If necessary, create a custom bridge network and attach your containers to it. Verify that the containers are correctly referencing each other by container name or IP address.

Example:

```
bash

docker network ls
```

4. Permission Issues with Volumes

- **Cause**: Docker volumes may be mounted with incorrect permissions, preventing the container from reading or writing to the mounted volume.
- **Solution**: Check the permissions of the host directory or volume being mounted using `docker exec` to inspect the mounted directory inside the container. Use `chmod` or `chown` to fix the permissions if necessary.

Example:

```
bash

docker exec -it my-container ls -l /data
```

Debugging Multi-Container Applications

Debugging multi-container applications adds complexity because you need to troubleshoot interactions between different services.

Docker Compose is a common tool used for multi-container applications, and debugging these types of setups requires a few additional techniques.

1. Using `docker-compose logs` for Multi-Container Logs

With multi-container applications, you can view logs for all containers defined in the `docker-compose.yml` file using:

bash

```
docker-compose logs
```

You can also view logs for a specific service:

bash

```
docker-compose logs web
```

Use the `-f` option to follow logs in real-time:

bash

```
docker-compose logs -f
```

2. Accessing Logs of Specific Services

If your application is composed of multiple services (e.g., a web server, database, cache), check the logs of each service individually. For example, to see the logs for the database container, run:

```
bash
```

```
docker-compose logs db
```

3. Using Docker Compose for Container Interactions

Sometimes, containers need to interact with each other. If you are troubleshooting communication issues, you can use `docker-compose exec` to access a container's shell and test network connectivity with other containers.

For example, to access the `web` container and ping the `db` container:

```
bash
```

```
docker-compose exec web bash
ping db
```

This allows you to interactively test the connection between services within the Compose setup.

Performance Optimization Tips

Optimizing the performance of Docker containers is essential for ensuring your application runs efficiently in production. Here are some tips to improve the performance of Docker containers:

1. Minimize Image Size

Smaller images are faster to build, pull, and deploy. Here are a few ways to reduce the size of your Docker images:

- Use smaller base images (e.g., `alpine` instead of `ubuntu`).
- Clean up unnecessary dependencies after installing them in the Dockerfile.
- Use multi-stage builds to keep the final image small by discarding build dependencies.

2. Use Caching Effectively

Docker uses a build cache to optimize the image-building process. Ensure that you order the instructions in your Dockerfile so that frequently changing commands (like ing application files) come after stable commands (like installing dependencies). This allows Docker to reuse the cache for commands that haven't changed.

3. Optimize Resource Limits

Docker containers can consume significant resources (CPU, memory, and disk). Use the `--memory`, `--cpus`, and `--disk` flags to set resource limits for containers:

```bash
docker run --memory="256m" --cpus="1.0" my-container
```

This ensures that containers don't consume excessive resources and helps prevent them from negatively impacting the host system.

4. Use Volumes for Persistent Data

Avoid storing persistent data inside containers. Use Docker volumes to store data, as they are optimized for performance and can be easily backed up and migrated. Volumes also allow data to persist even if the container is removed.

5. Monitor Container Performance

Use Docker's built-in `docker stats` command to monitor real-time resource usage of containers:

```bash
```

```
docker stats
```

This will display the CPU, memory, and network usage of all running containers.

Summary:

In this chapter, we explored various methods for debugging and troubleshooting Docker containers. We covered how to use `docker logs`, `docker exec`, and `docker inspect` to gather information and debug issues. We also addressed common Docker issues, such as container crashes, port binding issues, and networking problems, along with their respective solutions. For multi-container applications, we discussed how to view logs using `docker-compose logs` and interact with containers using `docker-compose exec`. Finally, we provided performance optimization tips, such as minimizing image sizes, using caching effectively, and setting resource limits, to help you build more efficient and robust Docker containers.

CHAPTER 14

DOCKER IN PRODUCTION ENVIRONMENTS

Deploying Docker Containers in Production

Deploying Docker containers in a production environment involves setting up containers in a way that ensures high availability, scalability, and security. Docker's flexibility makes it a great choice for deploying applications in production, but there are several considerations to ensure everything runs smoothly.

1. Choosing the Right Deployment Platform

Docker can be deployed on a variety of platforms, including on-premise hardware, cloud providers (AWS, Azure, Google Cloud), and container orchestration platforms like Kubernetes. Depending on your needs, you can choose the right platform for managing Docker containers in production.

- **Standalone Docker Hosts**: For simple use cases, you can deploy Docker containers directly to a single host. This is typically suitable for small applications or testing environments but doesn't offer scalability and high availability.

- **Container Orchestration (e.g., Kubernetes, Docker Swarm)**: For larger applications, deploying containers via orchestration platforms is more efficient. Kubernetes and Docker Swarm provide features like automatic scaling, failover, service discovery, and load balancing, ensuring your containers can handle production traffic.

2. Using Docker Compose in Production

While Docker Compose is great for local development and testing, it's generally not recommended for production deployments that require high availability and scaling. Instead, Docker Compose can be used for managing smaller, less complex applications in production, especially in isolated environments or single-node setups.

For more robust environments, you should move to orchestration tools like **Kubernetes** or **Docker Swarm**. These tools can take over container management, scaling, load balancing, and fault tolerance.

3. Managing Persistent Data in Production

In production environments, it is critical to ensure that data is properly managed and persisted. Containers are ephemeral, meaning they can be stopped, started, or deleted at any time, and data inside containers can be lost.

- **Volumes**: Use Docker volumes to persist application data. Volumes are stored outside the container filesystem and ensure data persistence even if the container is stopped or removed.
- **Backup Strategies**: Regular backups of critical data (stored in volumes) are essential. Use automated backup solutions or integrate backup services that can handle Docker volumes.

Best Practices for Securing Docker Containers

Security is a top priority when deploying Docker containers in production environments. Docker provides several built-in features to help secure containers, but it's important to follow best practices to minimize potential vulnerabilities.

1. Run Containers as Non-Root Users

Running containers as the root user can lead to security risks if the container is compromised. By default, Docker containers run as the root user, but you should explicitly specify a non-root user in the `Dockerfile` to reduce security vulnerabilities.

To set a non-root user in a Dockerfile:

144

```
Dockerfile
```

```
USER appuser
```

2. Use Official and Trusted Images

Always use official Docker images or images from trusted sources. Official images are regularly updated, maintained, and tested for security vulnerabilities. Be cautious when using third-party images, especially those from unverified sources, as they may contain vulnerabilities or malicious code.

- Check the image for vulnerabilities using security scanning tools like **Anchore**, **Clair**, or **Trivy**.

3. Limit Container Privileges

Limit the privileges of containers by using Docker's security options, such as:

- `--cap-drop`: Drops unnecessary Linux capabilities from the container.
- `--security-opt`: Enables additional security features, such as **AppArmor** or **SELinux** profiles.

Example:

```bash
```

```
docker      run      --cap-drop=ALL      --security-opt
seccomp=unconfined my-container
```

4. Network Segmentation and Isolation

Use Docker's network features to isolate containers and reduce exposure to potential attacks. Docker provides different network modes like `bridge`, `host`, and `overlay`. In a production environment, create isolated networks for different services to prevent unauthorized access.

For example, a web application should be isolated from a database container on a different network.

```
bash
```

```
docker      network      create      --driver      bridge
isolated_network
```

5. Regularly Update Docker and Containers

Ensure that both Docker and the container images you use are up-to-date with the latest security patches. This includes regularly updating your Docker Engine and periodically rebuilding containers from base images to incorporate the latest patches.

Resource Limits and CPU Allocation for Containers

Containers are lightweight, but they still consume system resources. When deploying Docker containers in production, it's important to allocate system resources such as CPU, memory, and disk space to ensure that containers perform optimally without overwhelming the host system.

1. Setting CPU and Memory Limits

You can set resource limits for Docker containers to prevent them from consuming excessive resources. Use the `--memory` and `--cpus` options to control how much memory and CPU a container can use.

- **Memory Limit**: Restricts the amount of memory the container can use.

  Example:

  ```bash
  ```

  ```
  docker run --memory="512m" my-container
  ```

- **CPU Limit**: Limits the CPU usage of the container.

  Example:

  ```bash
  ```

147

```
docker run --cpus="1.5" my-container
```

This ensures that no single container can monopolize the host machine's resources.

2. Using CPU Shares

Instead of setting an absolute CPU limit, you can use **CPU shares** to control the relative priority of containers when CPU resources are under pressure. The higher the CPU share value, the more CPU the container will receive.

Example:

```
bash
```

```
docker run --cpu-shares=512 my-container
```

By default, all containers have a CPU share value of 1024, and containers with higher values will receive more CPU time when the system is under load.

3. Disk I/O Limits

You can also set limits on disk I/O usage for containers using the `--blkio-weight` option, which controls the block I/O weight (I/O priority) of the container.

148

Example:

```
bash

docker run --blkio-weight=500 my-container
```

Setting disk I/O limits ensures that one container doesn't overwhelm the disk performance and degrade the performance of other containers.

Setting Up Monitoring and Logging for Docker Containers

To ensure that Docker containers run smoothly in production, monitoring and logging are essential. Docker provides several tools for monitoring the performance of containers and collecting logs for troubleshooting.

1. Setting Up Docker Monitoring

To monitor Docker containers in production, you can use a variety of monitoring tools that collect and visualize metrics related to CPU, memory, disk I/O, and network usage.

Popular monitoring tools for Docker:

- **Prometheus**: Open-source monitoring and alerting toolkit. It can collect and store time-series data about container performance.

- **Grafana**: A powerful visualization tool often used alongside Prometheus to create dashboards and graphs to monitor Docker containers.
- **cAdvisor**: A lightweight tool by Google to monitor the resource usage of containers.

Example of running **cAdvisor** in a container:

bash

```
docker run -d --name=cadvisor --volume=/var/run/docker.sock:/var/run/docker.sock --publish=8080:8080 google/cadvisor:latest
```

This runs cAdvisor and exposes a web interface on port 8080 to monitor container performance.

2. Setting Up Docker Logging

By default, Docker logs output to the container's standard output and standard error streams. These logs can be accessed using the `docker logs` command.

To ensure that logs are captured and persisted for analysis, Docker supports different logging drivers. The most common logging driver for production environments is **json-file**, but you can use others like **syslog**, **fluentd**, or **journald** for better integration with centralized logging systems.

Example of configuring a logging driver in Docker Compose:

```yaml
version: '3'

services:
  web:
    image: my-web-app
    logging:
      driver: "json-file"
      options:
        max-size: "10m"
        max-file: "3"
```

This configuration ensures that logs for the web service are stored in a JSON format, with log files limited to a maximum size of 10 MB and up to 3 rotated log files.

3. Centralized Logging with ELK Stack or EFK Stack

For larger production environments, it's a good idea to set up centralized logging. The **ELK Stack** (Elasticsearch, Logstash, and Kibana) or **EFK Stack** (Elasticsearch, Fluentd, and Kibana) are popular solutions for aggregating, searching, and visualizing Docker container logs.

- **Logstash/Fluentd** collects logs from Docker containers and forwards them to **Elasticsearch**, which stores and indexes the logs.
- **Kibana** is used to visualize the logs in real-time via a web interface.

Summary:

In this chapter, we discussed how to deploy Docker containers in production environments while ensuring high availability, security, and performance. We covered best practices for securing containers, such as running them as non-root users, using trusted images, and limiting privileges. We also discussed setting resource limits, including memory, CPU, and disk I/O limits, to ensure containers don't consume excessive resources. Additionally, we explored how to monitor Docker containers using tools like **Prometheus**, **Grafana**, and **cAdvisor**, as well as how to manage logs using different logging drivers and centralized logging solutions like the **ELK** or **EFK** stack. These practices ensure that your Docker containers perform optimally and remain secure in a production environment.

CHAPTER 15

DOCKER SWARM: NATIVE CLUSTERING AND ORCHESTRATION

Introduction to Docker Swarm and Clustering

Docker Swarm is Docker's native clustering and orchestration tool. It allows you to group multiple Docker hosts (physical or virtual machines) into a **cluster**. This cluster, known as a **Swarm**, is managed as a single virtual Docker engine, providing high availability, load balancing, and scalability for containerized applications. Swarm mode is Docker's built-in solution for orchestrating containers and services across multiple hosts.

Key Features of Docker Swarm:

- **Clustering**: Swarm turns a collection of Docker engines into a single, unified cluster, enabling containers to be distributed across different machines.
- **High Availability**: Docker Swarm provides built-in redundancy and fault tolerance. If a node (host machine)

153

fails, Swarm will automatically reschedule tasks (containers) to healthy nodes.

- **Load Balancing**: Swarm mode can automatically distribute traffic across containers running on different nodes in the cluster, ensuring efficient resource usage.

- **Declarative Service Model**: You can define the desired state of your application using a service, and Docker Swarm will ensure that this state is maintained (e.g., maintaining a specified number of replicas).

- **Scaling**: Docker Swarm allows you to easily scale services up or down by adjusting the number of replicas (instances) running for each service.

Docker Swarm is ideal for teams who need to manage containers across multiple machines without relying on more complex orchestrators like Kubernetes.

Setting Up a Docker Swarm Cluster

To get started with Docker Swarm, you need at least two Docker nodes: one **manager node** and one or more **worker nodes**. The manager node is responsible for managing the Swarm and distributing tasks, while worker nodes execute the tasks.

1. Initialize a Swarm Cluster

On the first node, you'll initialize the Docker Swarm using the `docker swarm init` command. This node will become the manager node.

bash

```
docker swarm init --advertise-addr <manager_ip>
```

- **--advertise-addr**: Specifies the IP address of the manager node. This is the address other nodes will use to join the Swarm.

Once the Swarm is initialized, Docker will output a join token that allows other nodes to join the Swarm as worker nodes. The output will look something like this:

bash

```
docker swarm join --token <worker_join_token> <manager_ip>:2377
```

2. Add Worker Nodes to the Swarm

On each worker node, run the `docker swarm join` command provided by the manager node. This command will add the node to the Swarm cluster.

bash

```
docker  swarm  join  --token  <worker_join_token>
<manager_ip>:2377
```

3. Verifying the Cluster

Once all the nodes have joined the Swarm, you can check the status of the cluster with the following command:

```
bash
```

```
docker node ls
```

This will display a list of all nodes in the Swarm, including the manager node and worker nodes, their status, and whether they are ready to accept tasks.

Scaling Services with Docker Swarm

One of the main benefits of Docker Swarm is the ability to scale applications easily. Docker Swarm allows you to specify the desired number of replicas (instances) of a service, and it will automatically create and distribute those replicas across the cluster.

1. Scaling a Service

To scale a service in Docker Swarm, you define the number of replicas you want in the service's configuration and deploy it. For example, if you have a service that you want to run in 3 replicas, you can scale it like this:

```bash
docker service scale <service_name>=3
```

This will ensure that 3 replicas of the service are running across the Swarm cluster. Docker Swarm will automatically distribute these replicas across the available nodes to maintain the desired number.

2. Automatically Adjusting Replica Count

You can also define scaling parameters at deployment using the `docker service create` command. For example, to create a service that starts with 3 replicas:

```bash
docker service create --name my-web-app --replicas 3 -p 8080:80 nginx
```

This command will create a new service named `my-web-app` running 3 replicas of the `nginx` container, each listening on port `8080` of the host machine.

3. Updating Service Scaling

If you want to change the scaling of a service (e.g., increase or decrease the number of replicas), you can do so with the following command:

```bash
docker service scale my-web-app=5
```

This will update the service to have 5 replicas. Swarm will automatically add or remove containers to meet the desired replica count.

Managing Services and Tasks in Swarm Mode

In Docker Swarm, **services** are the higher-level abstractions that define the desired state of an application, while **tasks** are the individual instances of containers running in the Swarm.

1. Viewing Services and Tasks

To view the services running in the Swarm, use the following command:

```bash
```

```bash
docker service ls
```

This will display a list of services, including the number of replicas, running tasks, and the current status.

To view detailed information about a specific service, including the running tasks, use:

```bash
```

```bash
docker service ps <service_name>
```

This will show the individual tasks (containers) running as part of the service, their current state (running, starting, etc.), and the nodes they are deployed on.

2. Updating Services

You can update a service in Swarm mode by changing its configuration or image. For example, to update the `nginx` image for the `my-web-app` service:

```
bash
```

```
docker service update --image nginx:latest my-
web-app
```

This will update the service to use the latest version of the `nginx` image, and Docker Swarm will automatically replace the old containers with the new ones in a rolling update fashion, ensuring no downtime.

3. Removing Services

To remove a service from the Swarm, use the following command:

```
bash
```

```
docker service rm <service_name>
```

This will remove the service and stop all associated containers.

Handling Task Failures and Recovery

Docker Swarm ensures high availability and fault tolerance by rescheduling tasks (containers) that fail or get removed. If a container stops, Docker Swarm will automatically deploy a new one on an available node to replace it, based on the service's configuration.

160

1. Inspecting Task Failures

To see the logs of a failed task, you can use the `docker service ps` command:

```bash
docker service ps <service_name>
```

This will show the status of each task, including any failures. If a task is failing, you can inspect the container logs to diagnose the issue.

2. Draining Nodes

If you need to temporarily remove a node from the cluster (for maintenance or other reasons), you can "drain" the node, which will stop scheduling new tasks on it. The tasks currently running on the node will be rescheduled to other nodes in the Swarm.

```bash
docker node update --availability drain <node_name>
```

After the maintenance is complete, you can bring the node back into the cluster:

```bash
bash
```

```
docker    node    update    --availability    active
<node_name>
```

Summary:

In this chapter, we covered Docker Swarm, Docker's native clustering and orchestration tool. We discussed how to set up a Docker Swarm cluster, including initializing a manager node, adding worker nodes, and verifying the cluster's status. We also explored how to scale services in Docker Swarm by adjusting the number of replicas, and how to manage services and tasks, such as viewing services, updating services, and removing them. Docker Swarm's built-in fault tolerance ensures that tasks are rescheduled automatically in case of failure. Additionally, we covered task failure recovery and how to drain nodes for maintenance. Docker Swarm makes it easy to deploy, manage, and scale containerized applications in a distributed environment.

CHAPTER 16

KUBERNETES VS. DOCKER SWARM: A COMPARISON

Key Differences Between Kubernetes and Docker Swarm

Docker Swarm and Kubernetes are both powerful container orchestration tools that allow you to manage containerized applications in a distributed environment. While both provide similar functionality, they have different approaches and feature sets. Understanding these key differences will help you determine which solution is best suited for your needs.

1. Architecture and Complexity

- **Docker Swarm**:
    - Docker Swarm is Docker's native container orchestration tool and is tightly integrated with Docker. It has a simpler architecture, making it easier to set up and use, especially for small to medium-scale applications.
    - **Swarm Mode**: Docker Swarm uses a manager-worker architecture. The manager node is responsible for orchestrating the swarm, while

163

worker nodes run the tasks (containers). Swarm mode is built into Docker, so no additional installation is required.

- o **Ease of Setup**: Swarm is designed to be simple, with fewer configuration steps compared to Kubernetes. It's a good choice for users already familiar with Docker.

- **Kubernetes**:

  - o Kubernetes has a more complex architecture and is typically used for large-scale applications. It includes multiple components such as the **API server**, **controller manager**, **scheduler**, and **etcd** (a distributed key-value store).

  - o **Master-Node Architecture**: Kubernetes uses a master node to manage and control the cluster, and worker nodes to run containers. It provides high availability and fault tolerance, making it suitable for enterprise-grade applications.

  - o **Complexity**: Kubernetes has a steeper learning curve and requires more setup, but it offers greater flexibility and scalability for complex, distributed systems.

2. Scalability

- **Docker Swarm**:

- o Swarm is designed for simplicity and is suitable for small to medium-scale applications. It can scale horizontally by adding more nodes to the cluster, but it's generally less feature-rich when it comes to scaling.
- o **Scaling Services**: You can scale services by adjusting the number of replicas, but advanced features like auto-scaling require manual setup or third-party tools.
- **Kubernetes**:
  - o Kubernetes is highly scalable and designed to handle complex, large-scale applications. It is ideal for massive clusters and cloud-native applications, offering features like **auto-scaling**, **horizontal pod scaling**, and **self-healing**.
  - o Kubernetes can automatically scale the number of containers (pods) based on resource usage or external metrics, such as CPU and memory.

3. Load Balancing

- **Docker Swarm**:
  - o Swarm includes **built-in load balancing**, which is simple to configure. It can automatically distribute traffic to containers based on the available replicas of a service.

o Swarm does not require a separate load balancer, making it simpler but less feature-rich in comparison to Kubernetes.

- **Kubernetes**:
  - o Kubernetes also provides load balancing but is more flexible. It supports **in-cluster load balancing** using services like **ClusterIP**, **NodePort**, and **LoadBalancer**. It also integrates well with cloud providers for external load balancing (e.g., AWS ELB, Google Cloud Load Balancing).
  - o Kubernetes allows more granular control over traffic routing and load balancing for complex services.

4. Networking

- **Docker Swarm**:
  - o Docker Swarm uses **overlay networks** to connect containers running on different hosts. It's simpler to set up, but its networking capabilities are more basic compared to Kubernetes.
  - o Swarm's networking is more straightforward, making it a good option for simple applications with fewer network requirements.
- **Kubernetes**:

166

- o Kubernetes provides more advanced networking capabilities, such as **Pod networking** and **network policies**. Kubernetes supports **Calico**, **Flannel**, and other CNI (Container Network Interface) plugins for flexible networking.
- o Kubernetes networking is more complex, but it provides more control over traffic flow and policies.

5. Ecosystem and Extensibility

- **Docker Swarm**:
  - o Swarm has fewer features and tools in its ecosystem but is tightly integrated with Docker, making it easier for users familiar with Docker to get started.
  - o Swarm's extensibility is limited compared to Kubernetes, but it supports basic features like volumes, services, and networking.
- **Kubernetes**:
  - o Kubernetes has a rich ecosystem with tools for monitoring (e.g., Prometheus), logging (e.g., ELK stack), CI/CD (e.g., Helm), and networking (e.g., Istio).
  - o Kubernetes is highly extensible, allowing users to integrate custom tools, third-party services, and add-ons.

When to Choose Docker Swarm Over Kubernetes and Vice Versa

Choosing between Docker Swarm and Kubernetes depends on the complexity and scale of your application, as well as your team's experience with container orchestration tools.

When to Choose Docker Swarm:

- **Small to Medium-Scale Applications**: Swarm is well-suited for simpler applications or projects with fewer containers. It's easier to set up and manage, making it ideal for small teams or applications that don't require complex orchestration.

- **Simplicity and Speed**: Swarm is quicker to deploy and configure, making it a good option if you need a fast, lightweight solution for container orchestration without the overhead of learning a complex system like Kubernetes.

- **Docker-Centric Workflow**: If your team is already familiar with Docker and you want to use a container orchestration tool that's fully integrated with Docker, Docker Swarm is a natural choice.

When to Choose Kubernetes:

- **Large-Scale Applications**: Kubernetes is ideal for complex, large-scale applications that require high availability, automatic scaling, and fault tolerance. If your application needs to scale horizontally, manage hundreds or thousands of containers, or handle complex traffic routing, Kubernetes is the better option.

- **Advanced Features**: If you need advanced features like auto-scaling, rolling updates, persistent storage management, and integrated service discovery, Kubernetes offers the flexibility and power needed for enterprise-level container orchestration.

- **Cloud-Native Applications**: Kubernetes is the go-to solution for cloud-native applications, especially those built with microservices in mind. It's deeply integrated with cloud platforms like AWS, Google Cloud, and Azure, allowing you to leverage cloud-native features like dynamic scaling, resource allocation, and managed services.

Use Cases for Both Docker Swarm and Kubernetes

Use Cases for Docker Swarm:

- **Small to Medium Projects**: Swarm is suitable for startups or small businesses that need simple orchestration without the complexity of Kubernetes.
- **Microservices with Basic Requirements**: If your microservices architecture doesn't require complex networking, persistent storage, or dynamic scaling, Docker Swarm is an excellent choice.
- **Dev/Test Environments**: Docker Swarm is great for local development and testing environments where speed and simplicity are more important than scalability.

Use Cases for Kubernetes:

- **Enterprise-Scale Applications**: Kubernetes excels in large, distributed environments where applications need to be highly available, scalable, and resilient.
- **Microservices Architectures**: Kubernetes is the preferred tool for managing microservices-based applications that require dynamic scaling, complex service discovery, and high availability.
- **Cloud-Native Applications**: Kubernetes is designed to run in the cloud and is tightly integrated with cloud platforms. It's the go-to choice for cloud-native applications and hybrid cloud deployments.

- **Applications with High Security and Compliance Needs**: Kubernetes has robust security features, such as role-based access control (RBAC), network policies, and secrets management, making it a strong choice for applications that require high levels of security and compliance.

High-Level Overview of Kubernetes Architecture

Kubernetes has a modular, microservice-oriented architecture that is designed to provide scalable and resilient container orchestration. Below is an overview of the key components of Kubernetes architecture:

1. Master Node (Control Plane):

The **master node** is responsible for managing the Kubernetes cluster and making global decisions, such as scheduling, scaling, and monitoring the health of the cluster. It contains several key components:

- **API Server**: The API server exposes the Kubernetes API and serves as the entry point for all commands and requests. It acts as a proxy between the user and the cluster.

- **Controller Manager**: The controller manager ensures that the desired state of the cluster is maintained by continuously monitoring the cluster's state and performing necessary actions (e.g., scaling, health checks).

- **Scheduler**: The scheduler is responsible for assigning tasks (pods) to available worker nodes in the cluster.

- **etcd**: A distributed key-value store that holds the configuration data and the state of the cluster, including information about nodes, pods, and services.

2. Worker Nodes (Nodes):

Worker nodes are the machines (physical or virtual) that run the actual workloads (containers). Each node in the Kubernetes cluster contains several key components:

- **Kubelet**: The kubelet is an agent that runs on each node and ensures that containers are running as expected. It communicates with the master node and reports the status of containers.

- **Kube Proxy**: The kube proxy manages network traffic between services and handles load balancing, ensuring that requests are routed to the correct pod or service.

- **Container Runtime**: The container runtime is responsible for running containers. Kubernetes supports multiple container runtimes, such as Docker, containerd, and CRI-O.

3. Pods:

A **pod** is the smallest and simplest unit in Kubernetes. It represents a single instance of a running process in the cluster and may contain one or more containers that share the same network namespace, storage volumes, and other resources.

4. Services:

Kubernetes services define how to access a set of pods and enable communication between containers. They provide load balancing, DNS resolution, and service discovery for containers running in the cluster.

Summary:

In this chapter, we compared **Docker Swarm** and **Kubernetes**, highlighting their key differences in architecture, scalability, load balancing, networking, and extensibility. We discussed when to choose Docker Swarm over Kubernetes and vice versa, depending on your application's complexity and requirements. Docker Swarm is ideal for simpler, smaller-scale applications, while Kubernetes excels in large-scale, cloud-native, and enterprise applications. We also provided a high-level overview of Kubernetes architecture, including its master node, worker nodes, pods, and services, and explained how Kubernetes provides advanced features for managing containers at scale.

CHAPTER 17

DOCKER NETWORKING IN CLUSTERS

Overlay Networks and Docker Swarm

Docker Swarm leverages **overlay networks** to enable communication between containers running on different Docker hosts (nodes) in a Swarm cluster. Overlay networks abstract the physical network and create a virtual network that spans multiple nodes, allowing containers to communicate across machines in the cluster as if they were on the same host.

How Overlay Networks Work:

- **VXLAN Tunneling**: Overlay networks in Docker Swarm use **VXLAN (Virtual Extensible LAN)** tunneling to encapsulate network traffic and create a virtual network across multiple Docker hosts. VXLAN allows Docker containers running on different hosts to communicate securely.

- **Network Isolation**: Containers on overlay networks are isolated from containers on other networks, providing security and preventing unauthorized access. You can

175

define which containers or services can communicate with each other by placing them on different networks.

- **Swarm Node Communication**: Docker Swarm automatically handles the management of overlay networks when you deploy services. It ensures that containers are able to communicate with each other even when they are running on different nodes in the cluster.

Benefits of Overlay Networks in Docker Swarm:

- **Multi-Host Communication**: Overlay networks allow containers on different Swarm nodes to communicate seamlessly.
- **Network Isolation**: You can isolate containers and services by placing them on different networks, ensuring security and better traffic control.
- **Scalability**: As the Swarm cluster grows, overlay networks ensure that communication is possible between all containers regardless of the physical host they are on.

Example: Creating an Overlay Network in Docker Swarm:

To create an overlay network in Docker Swarm, use the `docker network create` command with the `--driver overlay` option.

`bash`

```
docker    network    create    --driver    overlay
my_overlay_network
```

Once the network is created, you can deploy services that use this network:

```bash
bash

docker service create --name my-service --network
my_overlay_network nginx
```

This command creates a service (`my-service`) and connects it to the `my_overlay_network` overlay network.

Setting Up Custom Networks in Docker Swarm

Docker Swarm allows you to set up custom networks to control how containers communicate with each other and the outside world. These networks can be used to define service communication rules, set up security policies, and provide different types of connectivity.

1. Creating Custom Networks in Docker Swarm

You can create custom networks in Docker Swarm using the `docker network create` command with the desired network driver (`overlay`, `bridge`, etc.). Custom networks give you more control over network configuration and service connectivity.

For example, to create a custom overlay network for Docker Swarm:

bash

```
docker network create --driver overlay --scope swarm my_custom_network
```

- **`--driver overlay`**: Specifies the overlay driver, which allows for communication between containers across different nodes in the Swarm.
- **`--scope swarm`**: Ensures the network is available to services in the Swarm cluster.

2. Connecting Services to Custom Networks

Once the network is created, you can specify it when creating services in Docker Swarm. For example:

bash

```
docker service create --name web --network my_custom_network nginx
```

This command creates a `web` service and connects it to the `my_custom_network` network.

178

3. Using Multiple Networks in Docker Swarm

You can also connect services to multiple networks. This is useful if you want to isolate certain traffic while allowing services to communicate across networks. For example:

```bash
docker service create --name web --network my_custom_network --network my_other_network nginx
```

This command connects the `web` service to both `my_custom_network` and `my_other_network`.

Service Discovery and Load Balancing in Docker Swarm

One of the key benefits of Docker Swarm is **built-in service discovery** and **load balancing**. Swarm makes it easy for containers to find and communicate with each other, even as they are distributed across multiple nodes in the cluster.

1. Service Discovery

Service discovery in Docker Swarm allows containers to communicate with each other by using **service names** rather than IP addresses. Swarm automatically assigns a DNS name to each service in the cluster, which can be used by containers to find and communicate with other services.

For example, if you create a service called web, you can access it from another service using the service name web:

bash

```
docker service create --name web nginx
docker service create --name api --network
my_overlay_network --env WEB_HOST=web my-api-
image
```

In this example, the api service can access the web service by simply referencing web as the hostname, and Docker Swarm will resolve this name to the appropriate container's IP address.

2. Load Balancing

Docker Swarm automatically provides load balancing for services. When you deploy a service with multiple replicas, Swarm will distribute incoming traffic evenly across the replicas.

When a client sends a request to a service, Docker Swarm's internal load balancer routes the request to one of the available container instances (replicas). The load balancing is handled automatically without the need for manual configuration.

For example, if you have a service called web with 3 replicas:

```
bash

docker service create --name web --replicas 3
nginx
```

Docker Swarm automatically load balances traffic between the 3 replicas, ensuring high availability and efficient resource utilization.

Using DNS in Docker Networks

Docker uses **DNS (Domain Name System)** for service discovery in containers. When you run a container within a Docker network, it can resolve the names of other services and containers on the same network using DNS.

1. Docker's Built-in DNS Resolution

By default, Docker provides an internal DNS server to handle service name resolution. Each service created within Docker Swarm is assigned a DNS name that can be used by other containers within the same network. This allows containers to communicate with each other by service name, rather than using static IP addresses.

For example, consider the following services:

- A web service running on an overlay network.

- A db service running on the same overlay network.

The web container can access the db container by simply using db as the hostname:

bash

```
docker   service   create   --name   web   --network
my_overlay_network nginx
docker   service   create   --name   db   --network
my_overlay_network mysql
```

Inside the web container, you can access the db service with:

bash

```
ping db
```

Docker will automatically resolve db to the correct container's IP address.

2. Custom DNS Configuration

You can configure custom DNS settings in Docker by passing DNS server addresses to the container when running or by setting DNS options in the `docker-compose.yml` file. This can be useful if your application needs to connect to external services outside the Docker network.

182

Example:

```bash
docker run --dns 8.8.8.8 my-container
```

This sets Google's DNS server as the DNS resolver for the container.

Summary:

In this chapter, we covered Docker networking in clusters, with a focus on overlay networks in Docker Swarm. Overlay networks allow containers to communicate across multiple Docker nodes, providing network isolation and simplifying multi-host communication. We discussed how to set up custom networks in Docker Swarm, how to manage service discovery and load balancing within Swarm, and how DNS is used for resolving service names. Docker Swarm's built-in networking features make it a powerful tool for managing multi-container applications in a distributed environment, ensuring that containers can communicate with each other seamlessly and reliably.

CHAPTER 18

SECURING DOCKER CONTAINERS

Security Best Practices for Docker Containers

Securing Docker containers is a critical step in ensuring that your applications run safely and are protected from potential threats. Containers share the underlying host OS, and a security vulnerability in one container could potentially affect other containers or the host system. To mitigate these risks, it's important to follow security best practices when using Docker in development and production environments.

1. Use Minimal Base Images

- Use **official and minimal base images** to reduce the attack surface. Minimal images, such as `alpine`, contain only the essential components required to run your application, which decreases the number of potential vulnerabilities.
- Regularly update your base images to incorporate security patches and fixes. Vulnerabilities in base images can

propagate to your containers, so it's crucial to stay up to date.

Example:

```
Dockerfile
```

```
FROM alpine:latest
```

2. Avoid Running Containers as Root

Running containers as the **root user** inside the container exposes your system to security risks. If an attacker gains access to the container, they will have full control over the container and potentially the host machine.

- **Use a Non-Root User**: Always configure your containers to run as non-root users. You can set this in your Dockerfile using the USER instruction.

Example:

```
Dockerfile
```

```
RUN adduser -D myuser
USER myuser
```

3. Minimize Container Privileges

- **Limit capabilities**: Containers run with a set of Linux capabilities. Docker allows you to drop unnecessary capabilities to reduce the potential attack surface. Use the --cap-drop flag to drop all or unnecessary capabilities.

Example:

bash

```
docker run --cap-drop=ALL my-container
```

- **Use --no-new-privileges**: This flag ensures that no process within the container can gain new privileges during its runtime, preventing privilege escalation.

bash

```
docker run --no-new-privileges my-container
```

4. Limit Container Resources

Limit the resources (CPU, memory, disk I/O) that containers can use. This can help prevent denial-of-service attacks that might occur if a container consumes excessive resources.

bash

```
docker run --memory="512m" --cpus="1.0" my-container
```

This limits the container to 512MB of memory and 1 CPU core.

186

5. Avoid Exposing Unnecessary Ports

Only expose the ports that are necessary for your application. Exposing unnecessary ports increases the attack surface by making additional entry points available.

Example:

bash

```
docker run -p 8080:80 my-container
```

This command only exposes port 80 of the container to port 8080 on the host, reducing unnecessary access points.

Managing Secrets and Sensitive Data

Managing secrets (such as passwords, API keys, and certificates) is a critical aspect of securing Docker containers. Docker provides several ways to handle sensitive data securely.

1. Use Docker Secrets for Sensitive Data

Docker Swarm includes a **secrets management** system that allows you to securely store and manage sensitive data such as passwords and private keys. Secrets are stored in the Swarm manager and only made available to the services that need them.

- **Storing Secrets**: Use the `docker secret create` command to store secrets.

Example:

```bash
```

```
echo "my_secret_password" | docker secret create
db_password -
```

- **Using Secrets in Services**: When creating a service, you can reference the secret and make it available to the container as a file mounted in `/run/secrets`.

Example:

```bash
```

```
docker service create --name my-service --secret
db_password my-image
```

This ensures that the sensitive data (e.g., `db_password`) is securely available to the container.

2. Avoid Storing Secrets in Dockerfiles or Environment Variables

Do not store secrets directly in your Dockerfile or as environment variables, as they can be easily extracted from images or container metadata.

- **Environment Variables**: Avoid putting secrets directly in the ENV directive in the Dockerfile. Instead, pass secrets securely at runtime.

Example:

```bash
```

```
docker run -e DB_PASSWORD="secret_password" my-container
```

This method is not recommended for sensitive data as the environment variables could be accessed by anyone with access to the container's metadata.

3. Use External Secrets Management Systems

For more advanced use cases, you can integrate Docker with external secrets management systems like **HashiCorp Vault**, **AWS Secrets Manager**, or **Azure Key Vault**. These systems provide additional security features, such as dynamic secrets, access policies, and audit logging.

Running Docker Containers as Non-Root Users

By default, Docker containers run as the root user, which can pose security risks if the container is compromised. To mitigate these risks, you should configure Docker containers to run as non-root users.

1. Create a Non-Root User in Dockerfile

You can create a user within the container by using the USER instruction in your Dockerfile. This ensures that the container runs with limited privileges, reducing the attack surface.

Example:

```
Dockerfile

RUN useradd -m appuser
USER appuser
```

This Dockerfile creates a user appuser and switches to that user, so the container doesn't run as root.

2. Docker Run User Option

When running a container, you can specify the user under which the container will execute using the --user flag.

Example:

```
bash

docker run --user appuser my-container
```

190

This ensures that the container runs as `appuser` instead of root.

Security Features of Docker: Docker Content Trust and User Namespaces

Docker includes several built-in security features designed to help secure your containers and images.

1. Docker Content Trust (DCT)

Docker Content Trust is a security feature that ensures images are signed and verified before they are pushed or pulled. This prevents the use of unverified or tampered images.

- **Enabling Docker Content Trust**:

   You can enable Docker Content Trust by setting the `DOCKER_CONTENT_TRUST` environment variable to `1`. This ensures that all images pushed or pulled are signed and verified.

   bash

   ```
   export DOCKER_CONTENT_TRUST=1
   ```

With this setting, Docker will verify the authenticity of images before they are used, preventing the use of potentially malicious images.

2. User Namespaces

Docker's **user namespaces** feature allows you to map the root user in a container to a non-root user on the host system. This increases the security of Docker containers by reducing the risk of privilege escalation from within the container.

- **Enabling User Namespaces**:

  You can enable user namespaces in Docker by editing the Docker configuration file (`/etc/docker/daemon.json`).

  Example:

  ```json
  {
    "userns-remap": "default"
  }
  ```

  This configuration ensures that the root user inside the container is mapped to a non-privileged user on the host system.

- **Benefits of User Namespaces**:
  - **Isolation**: Even if an attacker gains root access inside the container, they are limited to a non-privileged user on the host system, reducing the risk of compromise.
  - **Safer Multi-Tenancy**: In multi-tenant environments, user namespaces ensure that containers from different users or teams cannot interfere with each other's host system resources.

Summary:

In this chapter, we explored various security best practices for Docker containers, including using minimal base images, running containers as non-root users, and minimizing container privileges. We also discussed managing secrets and sensitive data, using Docker secrets for secure storage, and integrating external secrets management systems. Docker's security features, such as **Docker Content Trust** (DCT) and **user namespaces**, provide additional layers of protection for containerized applications. By following these best practices, you can significantly reduce the attack surface of your Docker containers and ensure that your containerized applications are secure in both development and production environments.

CHAPTER 19

MONITORING DOCKER CONTAINERS

Tools for Monitoring Docker Containers (Prometheus, Grafana)

Monitoring the performance and health of Docker containers is essential for maintaining high availability and ensuring the smooth operation of your applications. Several tools are available for tracking resource usage, identifying bottlenecks, and setting up alerts for potential issues.

1. Prometheus

Prometheus is an open-source monitoring and alerting toolkit that collects time-series data and is widely used for monitoring containers, including Docker. It scrapes metrics from Docker containers and stores them in its time-series database, providing powerful query capabilities to analyze and visualize container performance.

- **How Prometheus Works with Docker**:
  - Prometheus uses **exporters** to collect metrics from different sources. The **cAdvisor** exporter

is commonly used with Docker to gather container metrics such as CPU, memory, network, and disk usage.

o Prometheus queries these metrics and stores them, making it easy to create custom dashboards and alerts based on container performance.

• **Setting Up Prometheus with Docker**: To get started with Prometheus and Docker, you need to run Prometheus and the cAdvisor exporter as containers. Here's an example `docker-compose.yml` file to set up both Prometheus and cAdvisor:

```yaml
version: '3'
services:
  cadvisor:
    image: google/cadvisor:latest
    container_name: cadvisor
    ports:
      - "8080:8080"
    volumes:
      - /:/rootfs:ro
      - /var/run:/var/run:ro
      - /sys:/sys:ro
      -
/var/lib/docker/:/var/lib/docker:ro
```

195

```
prometheus:
    image: prom/prometheus
    container_name: prometheus
    ports:
        - "9090:9090"
    volumes:
        -
./prometheus.yml:/etc/prometheus/promethe
us.yml
    depends_on:
        - cadvisor
```

The above `docker-compose.yml` file sets up both **cAdvisor** and **Prometheus**:

- o **cAdvisor** collects and exposes container metrics.
- o **Prometheus** scrapes metrics from cAdvisor and stores them.
- **Visualizing Metrics with Prometheus**: You can query Prometheus metrics directly from its web UI (available at `http://localhost:9090`), or use Grafana to create dashboards that visualize the data.

2. Grafana

Grafana is a popular open-source tool used for creating interactive and customizable dashboards to visualize metrics collected by Prometheus (or other monitoring tools). It integrates seamlessly with Prometheus to display Docker container metrics in real-time.

- **Setting Up Grafana with Prometheus**: To set up Grafana with Prometheus, you need to configure Grafana to use Prometheus as a data source. After that, you can create dashboards to visualize Docker container performance metrics.

- **Example of Using Grafana with Prometheus**: Here's a simple example of setting up a Grafana container to visualize metrics from Prometheus:

yaml

```yaml
version: '3'
services:
  grafana:
    image: grafana/grafana:latest
    container_name: grafana
    ports:
      - "3000:3000"
    environment:
      - GF_SECURITY_ADMIN_PASSWORD=admin
    depends_on:
      - prometheus
```

After setting up Grafana and Prometheus, you can log in to Grafana at `http://localhost:3000` and configure Prometheus as a data source. You can then create custom dashboards to visualize metrics such as CPU usage, memory usage, and disk I/O for your Docker containers.

- **Pre-built Dashboards**: Grafana provides pre-built dashboards for Docker and Prometheus, which can be imported directly from the Grafana website or community contributions.

Using `docker stats` to Track Resource Usage

Docker provides a simple built-in command, `docker stats`, to view real-time performance metrics of your containers. This command displays container-specific resource usage, such as CPU, memory, network, and disk usage.

1. Basic Usage of `docker stats`

To see the resource usage of all running containers:

```bash
```

```
docker stats
```

This command shows a live stream of the following resource metrics for each container:

- **CPU**: The percentage of CPU the container is using.

198

- **MEMORY**: The memory usage, including the percentage of memory.
- **NET I/O**: The amount of data sent and received by the container over the network.
- **BLOCK I/O**: The amount of data read from and written to the container's disk.
- **PIDS**: The number of processes running inside the container.

2. Monitoring Specific Containers

You can also monitor specific containers by specifying the container IDs or names:

bash

```
docker stats <container_name_or_id>
```

This will display the stats for just the specified container, which is useful when you want to focus on one service or container.

3. Using docker stats for Historical Data

docker stats shows real-time data, but if you want to capture historical metrics for analysis, consider integrating Docker with Prometheus or another external monitoring tool. Docker stats is useful for quick diagnostics but lacks persistent data storage.

Setting Up Alerts and Logs for Container Health

Setting up **alerts** and **logs** for container health is crucial for proactively managing containerized applications. Docker containers can fail or encounter performance issues, and setting up alerts will help notify you when these issues arise.

1. Setting Up Alerts in Prometheus

Prometheus has a powerful alerting system that can be configured using alerting rules. Alerts are triggered based on predefined conditions, such as CPU usage exceeding a threshold or container memory usage reaching a critical level.

To set up an alert in Prometheus, add an alert rule to your `prometheus.yml` configuration file:

yaml

```
groups:
  - name: container_alerts
    rules:
      - alert: HighCpuUsage
        expr:
sum(rate(container_cpu_usage_seconds_total{job=
"cadvisor"}[1m])) by (container_name) > 0.9
        for: 2m
        labels:
```

```
  severity: critical
annotations:
  summary: "Container CPU usage is high"
```

This rule triggers an alert if the CPU usage of any container exceeds 90% for more than 2 minutes. You can configure Prometheus to send notifications to **Alertmanager** and then forward them to Slack, email, or other alerting systems.

2. Logging with Docker

Docker supports various logging drivers to capture container logs, which can be stored in centralized logging systems. Common logging drivers include:

- **json-file**: The default logging driver, which stores logs in JSON format.
- **syslog**: Sends logs to a syslog server.
- **fluentd**: For integration with the Fluentd log collector.

Example of configuring the json-file logging driver in Docker:

```bash
docker run --log-driver=json-file my-container
```

3. Centralized Logging with ELK/EFK Stack

For more advanced log aggregation and analysis, you can use a logging stack like **ELK** (Elasticsearch, Logstash, Kibana) or **EFK** (Elasticsearch, Fluentd, Kibana).

- **Logstash** or **Fluentd** collect logs from Docker containers and forward them to **Elasticsearch**.
- **Kibana** is used to visualize and query logs.

Setting up the ELK or EFK stack can help you centralize logs from multiple containers, making it easier to search, analyze, and set up alerts based on log data.

Monitoring Multi-Container Applications

In a multi-container application, monitoring becomes more complex as you need to track resource usage and health across multiple services and containers. Tools like **Prometheus**, **Grafana**, and **cAdvisor** can provide a unified view of container health and resource consumption for all services in the application.

1. Prometheus and Multi-Container Monitoring

Prometheus can be set up to scrape metrics from all containers across your cluster. By using **labels** and **service discovery**, you can collect metrics from all the services running in your multi-container setup.

In Docker Swarm or Kubernetes, Prometheus can automatically discover services and containers, collecting metrics from each one.

Example of scraping metrics from multiple services in a Docker Swarm setup:

yaml

```
scrape_configs:
  - job_name: 'docker'
    static_configs:
      - targets: ['cadvisor:8080']
```

This configuration collects metrics from all containers exposed by **cAdvisor** in the Swarm, allowing you to track resource usage and health across your entire application.

2. Multi-Container Dashboards in Grafana

Grafana allows you to create dashboards that show metrics from multiple containers in a single view. This helps you monitor the health of the entire application, identify bottlenecks, and track key performance indicators (KPIs).

- You can use pre-built Grafana dashboards for Docker monitoring or customize your own to track metrics like:
  - **CPU usage** per container
  - **Memory usage** and **swap memory**
  - **Network I/O** per container
  - **Disk I/O** performance

These visualizations give you a comprehensive view of the health and performance of your multi-container applications.

Summary:

In this chapter, we covered the importance of monitoring Docker containers to ensure optimal performance and health in production environments. We discussed the use of tools like **Prometheus** and **Grafana** for collecting, visualizing, and alerting on container metrics. Docker's built-in command, `docker stats`, provides real-time resource usage statistics, but integrating Prometheus allows for more advanced monitoring and alerting. We also explored setting up centralized logging with tools like **ELK** or **EFK**, and discussed how to monitor multi-container applications in a Swarm or Kubernetes cluster. By implementing these monitoring practices, you can ensure the stability, performance, and security of your containerized applications.

CHAPTER 20

CONTINUOUS INTEGRATION AND DEPLOYMENT WITH DOCKER

Integrating Docker with CI/CD Pipelines

Continuous Integration (CI) and Continuous Deployment (CD) are essential practices for modern software development, enabling faster, more reliable delivery of applications. Docker plays a key role in CI/CD pipelines by providing a consistent and reproducible environment for building, testing, and deploying applications.

1. What is CI/CD?

- **Continuous Integration (CI)** involves automatically integrating code changes into a shared repository multiple times a day. CI ensures that changes do not break the application and that the codebase is always in a deployable state.

- **Continuous Deployment (CD)** extends CI by automating the deployment process. Whenever the code passes automated tests, it is automatically deployed to production or staging environments.

2. Why Use Docker in CI/CD?

- **Consistency**: Docker ensures that the development, testing, and production environments are consistent. By using Docker containers, developers and CI/CD systems can be sure that the application will run the same way in every environment.

- **Isolation**: Docker isolates dependencies within containers, so the application will not conflict with other applications or environments. This eliminates the "works on my machine" problem.

- **Portability**: Docker images can be easily transported across different stages of the pipeline, making it simple to move from testing to production environments without worrying about configuration issues.

Automating Builds and Tests Using Docker

Docker is a powerful tool for automating the building and testing of applications. By defining the application's environment in a `Dockerfile`, you can ensure that the build process is reproducible and consistent across all environments.

1. Automating Builds with Docker

In a CI pipeline, Docker images can be automatically built whenever code is committed to the repository. The process typically involves the following steps:

1. **Clone the Repository**: Pull the latest code from the version control system (e.g., Git).
2. **Build the Docker Image**: Use the `docker build` command to create a Docker image based on the `Dockerfile` in the repository.
3. **Push the Image**: After building the image, push it to a container registry (e.g., Docker Hub, AWS ECR, or a private registry) so it can be used in staging or production environments.

Example Docker build step in a CI pipeline:

```bash
docker build -t my-app:latest .
docker push my-app:latest
```

2. Automating Tests with Docker

Automated tests can be run inside Docker containers, providing a clean and consistent environment for testing. This ensures that the application is tested in an environment that closely matches production.

- **Unit Tests**: Run unit tests within the container to ensure that the code logic is correct.

- **Integration Tests**: Test the integration of different parts of the application within the container.

- **End-to-End Tests**: Run full application tests inside containers that simulate the entire workflow, ensuring that everything works together as expected.

Example of running tests in a Docker container:

```
bash
```

```
docker run --rm my-app:latest npm test
```

In this example, `npm test` runs inside the container to execute automated tests for a Node.js application.

Using Docker in Jenkins, GitLab, and GitHub Actions

Docker integrates seamlessly with popular CI/CD tools like **Jenkins**, **GitLab CI**, and **GitHub Actions**. These tools allow you to automate the process of building, testing, and deploying Docker containers in a reliable and repeatable manner.

1. Using Docker in Jenkins

Jenkins is one of the most widely used CI/CD tools. You can integrate Docker into Jenkins pipelines to build and test Docker images.

- **Jenkinsfile**: Define your CI/CD pipeline in a `Jenkinsfile` using Docker. Here's an example Jenkinsfile that builds a Docker image and runs tests:

```groovy
pipeline {
  agent any
  stages {
    stage('Build') {
      steps {
        script {
          docker.build('my-app')
        }
      }
    }
    stage('Test') {
      steps {
        script {
          docker.image('my-app').inside {
            sh 'npm test'
          }
        }
```

209

```
      }
    }
    stage('Deploy') {
      steps {
        script {
          // Deployment logic goes here
        }
      }
    }
  }
}
```

- **Docker in Jenkins Pipeline**: The `docker.build()` function builds the Docker image, and `docker.image().inside` runs the tests inside the container.

2. Using Docker in GitLab CI

GitLab CI is another popular tool for CI/CD that integrates well with Docker.

- **.gitlab-ci.yml**: The configuration file for GitLab CI, `.gitlab-ci.yml`, allows you to define stages for building, testing, and deploying your Docker containers.

Example `.gitlab-ci.yml` file:

yaml

```
stages:
    - build
    - test
    - deploy

build:
    stage: build
    script:
        - docker build -t my-app .

test:
    stage: test
    script:
        - docker run --rm my-app npm test

deploy:
    stage: deploy
    script:
        - docker push my-app
```

This file defines three stages: build, test, and deploy. Docker is used to build the image, run tests, and push the image to the registry.

3. Using Docker in GitHub Actions

GitHub Actions is a CI/CD tool built into GitHub that allows you to define workflows for automating tasks.

- **GitHub Actions Workflow**: In GitHub Actions, you define your CI/CD pipeline in a YAML file (`.github/workflows/ci.yml`).

Example GitHub Actions workflow:

```yaml
name: CI/CD Pipeline

on:
  push:
    branches:
      - main

jobs:
  build:
    runs-on: ubuntu-latest
    steps:
      - uses: actions/checkout@v2
      - name: Build Docker image
        run: docker build -t my-app .
      - name: Run tests
        run: docker run --rm my-app npm test
      - name: Push Docker image
        run: docker push my-app
```

This workflow automates the build, test, and deploy process using Docker.

212

Deploying Applications with Docker in a CI/CD Environment

Once Docker images have been built and tested, the next step in the CI/CD pipeline is deploying the application to a staging or production environment.

1. Docker in Production Deployments

In a CI/CD environment, Docker allows you to automate the deployment of applications to production or staging environments using the following methods:

- **Docker Compose**: For applications with multiple services (e.g., web server, database), you can use **Docker Compose** to define and deploy multi-container applications. The `docker-compose.yml` file defines the services, networks, and volumes, and `docker-compose up` brings the entire stack up in a production-like environment.

Example of deploying a multi-service application with Docker Compose:

bash

```
docker-compose up -d
```

- **Docker Swarm or Kubernetes**: For large-scale production environments, Docker Swarm or Kubernetes is used to orchestrate and manage the deployment of Docker containers across multiple nodes. These tools handle scaling, service discovery, and high availability for containerized applications.

2. Continuous Deployment with Docker

In continuous deployment (CD), whenever a change is pushed to the codebase and passes automated tests, the application is automatically deployed to production. Using Docker, you can automate the entire deployment process:

1. **Build Docker Image**: The CI pipeline builds the Docker image whenever there is a code change.
2. **Push Image to Registry**: After passing the tests, the image is pushed to a container registry (Docker Hub, AWS ECR, Google Container Registry, etc.).
3. **Deploy to Production**: The image is pulled from the registry and deployed to the production environment using Docker, Docker Swarm, or Kubernetes.

214

Summary:

In this chapter, we discussed how to integrate Docker with CI/CD pipelines to automate the build, test, and deployment of applications. We explored how Docker enhances the CI/CD process by providing a consistent and reproducible environment for all stages of development. We covered how to use Docker with popular CI/CD tools like **Jenkins**, **GitLab CI**, and **GitHub Actions**, and how Docker images are built, tested, and deployed in a CI/CD environment. By leveraging Docker in your CI/CD pipeline, you can achieve continuous integration, efficient testing, and seamless deployment of containerized applications.

CHAPTER 21

SCALING APPLICATIONS WITH DOCKER

Horizontal Scaling of Docker Containers

Horizontal scaling, also known as **scaling out**, refers to the process of adding more instances (or replicas) of a service to distribute the workload across multiple containers. Unlike **vertical scaling**, which involves increasing the resources (CPU, RAM) of a single container, horizontal scaling focuses on increasing the number of containers to improve performance, resilience, and availability.

How Horizontal Scaling Works in Docker

- **Docker Containers as Replicas**: In Docker, horizontal scaling is achieved by running multiple replicas of a containerized service. Docker Swarm and Kubernetes are both capable of managing multiple replicas of containers to ensure that applications can handle increased load by distributing traffic across multiple instances.

- **Service Management**: A service in Docker, whether in Swarm or Kubernetes, can be defined with a desired

216

number of replicas. Docker or Kubernetes will automatically ensure that the specified number of replicas is running and will distribute them across the available nodes in the cluster.

Example of Horizontal Scaling in Docker Swarm

In Docker Swarm, you can scale a service by specifying the number of replicas you want to run for a given service. For example, if you have a service named web and you want to scale it to 5 replicas:

bash

```
docker service scale web=5
```

This command will automatically create 5 replicas of the web service and distribute them across the available nodes in the Swarm.

Example of Horizontal Scaling in Kubernetes

In Kubernetes, scaling is done using the kubectl scale command. For example, to scale a deployment called my-web-app to 5 replicas:

bash

```
kubectl scale deployment my-web-app --replicas=5
```

This command instructs Kubernetes to ensure that there are 5 replicas of the `my-web-app` deployment running across the cluster.

Auto-Scaling in Docker Swarm and Kubernetes

Auto-scaling is the ability to automatically adjust the number of running containers based on real-time demand, such as traffic or resource usage (CPU, memory). Both **Docker Swarm** and **Kubernetes** provide mechanisms for auto-scaling containers to ensure that your application can handle varying traffic loads without manual intervention.

1. Auto-scaling in Docker Swarm

Docker Swarm supports **manual scaling** (as discussed earlier), but it does not have native support for **auto-scaling** based on load out of the box. However, you can implement auto-scaling by integrating Docker Swarm with external tools like **Prometheus** and **Alertmanager** to monitor metrics (e.g., CPU, memory usage) and trigger scaling actions.

To set up basic auto-scaling, you would need to create custom scripts or use an external monitoring tool to watch resource usage and then scale your services up or down based on predefined thresholds.

2. Auto-scaling in Kubernetes

Kubernetes provides built-in **Horizontal Pod Autoscaling (HPA)**, which automatically adjusts the number of pod replicas based on observed metrics like CPU usage or memory utilization. The HPA controller monitors resource consumption and scales the pods as needed to meet the target utilization.

Example of Setting Up Auto-scaling in Kubernetes:

To enable auto-scaling for a deployment in Kubernetes, you need to define an HPA object that specifies the scaling rules based on metrics like CPU usage.

```bash
kubectl autoscale deployment my-web-app --cpu-percent=50 --min=2 --max=10
```

This command sets up auto-scaling for the `my-web-app` deployment:

- **--cpu-percent=50**: Scale up or down to maintain 50% CPU usage per pod.
- **--min=2**: The minimum number of replicas.
- **--max=10**: The maximum number of replicas.

Kubernetes will now automatically adjust the number of replicas of `my-web-app` based on CPU usage, ensuring that the application can handle traffic spikes and scale down during periods of low demand.

Load Balancing and Managing Traffic

Load balancing is crucial for distributing incoming traffic across multiple replicas of a containerized service, ensuring that no single container is overwhelmed and that the application remains highly available.

1. Load Balancing in Docker Swarm

Docker Swarm has a built-in **load balancer** that automatically distributes traffic across the replicas of a service. When you expose a service via a port (e.g., HTTP port 80), Docker Swarm handles the routing of requests to the appropriate container instance.

For example, if you scale the `web` service to 3 replicas in Docker Swarm:

```bash
docker service scale web=3
```

Docker Swarm will automatically distribute incoming traffic across the 3 web service replicas, ensuring load balancing and high availability.

- **Internal Load Balancing**: Swarm uses a round-robin method to distribute traffic between containers within the Swarm.
- **External Load Balancing**: For traffic from outside the Swarm, you can use a reverse proxy like **Traefik** or **NGINX** to load balance requests across containers running in the Swarm.

2. Load Balancing in Kubernetes

Kubernetes also includes load balancing capabilities, but it provides more advanced options for managing traffic. Kubernetes uses **Services** to define how traffic should be routed to pods (containers). There are several types of services in Kubernetes:

- **ClusterIP**: Default service type that provides load balancing within the cluster.
- **NodePort**: Exposes the service on a specific port on each node in the cluster.
- **LoadBalancer**: Integrates with cloud provider load balancers (e.g., AWS ELB) to provide external load balancing.

- **Ingress**: Manages external HTTP(S) routing and load balancing.

Example of creating a Kubernetes service with load balancing:

bash

```
kubectl    expose    deployment    my-web-app    --
type=LoadBalancer --name=my-service
```

This command creates a Kubernetes service of type **LoadBalancer**, which routes traffic to the my-web-app pods and balances the load across them.

Handling Stateful Applications in a Containerized Environment

Stateful applications require persistent storage because they maintain data across restarts and scaling events. Docker and Kubernetes both provide mechanisms to handle stateful applications in a containerized environment, ensuring that data is preserved even if containers are stopped, moved, or rescheduled.

1. Docker Swarm and Stateful Applications

Docker Swarm supports persistent storage through **Docker volumes**. To manage stateful applications, you can use Docker volumes to store data outside the container, ensuring data persists even when containers are restarted or rescheduled.

To create a volume in Docker Swarm:

```bash
docker volume create my-data-volume
```

You can then use the volume in a service definition:

```bash
docker service create --name my-stateful-service
--mount                type=volume,source=my-data-
volume,target=/data my-stateful-image
```

This ensures that the `my-stateful-service` container uses the `my-data-volume` for persistent storage.

2. Kubernetes and Stateful Applications

Kubernetes provides more advanced support for stateful applications through **StatefulSets**. A **StatefulSet** ensures that each pod gets a unique, stable identifier and persistent storage that remains consistent even when pods are rescheduled.

- **Persistent Volumes (PVs)** and **Persistent Volume Claims (PVCs)** in Kubernetes allow for stateful data management by provisioning storage that survives pod restarts.

Example of creating a StatefulSet with persistent storage in Kubernetes:

yaml

```yaml
apiVersion: apps/v1
kind: StatefulSet
metadata:
  name: my-stateful-app
spec:
  serviceName: "my-stateful-app"
  replicas: 3
  selector:
    matchLabels:
      app: my-stateful-app
  template:
    metadata:
      labels:
        app: my-stateful-app
    spec:
      containers:
        - name: my-stateful-container
          image: my-stateful-image
          volumeMounts:
            - name: my-data-volume
              mountPath: /data
```

```
volumeClaimTemplates:
  - metadata:
      name: my-data-volume
    spec:
      accessModes: [ "ReadWriteOnce" ]
      resources:
        requests:
          storage: 1Gi
```

In this example:

- **StatefulSet** ensures that the pods have unique names and stable storage.
- **VolumeClaimTemplates** dynamically creates persistent volumes for each replica.

Kubernetes will ensure that each replica has access to its own persistent storage, making it ideal for stateful applications like databases.

Summary:

In this chapter, we covered the scaling capabilities of Docker, including **horizontal scaling** and **auto-scaling** in Docker Swarm and Kubernetes. Docker Swarm and Kubernetes both provide powerful mechanisms for scaling applications by adjusting the number of replicas based on demand. We also explored the **load**

balancing features in both Docker Swarm and Kubernetes, ensuring traffic is distributed across containers efficiently. Finally, we addressed how to handle **stateful applications** in Docker and Kubernetes by using volumes and StatefulSets, which ensure persistent storage and data consistency across containers in a containerized environment. By utilizing these scaling techniques, you can ensure your applications remain responsive and resilient, even under high demand.

CHAPTER 22

DOCKER FOR MICROSERVICES ARCHITECTURES

What is Microservices Architecture?

Microservices architecture is an approach to designing software systems where the application is split into multiple smaller, loosely coupled services. Each service represents a distinct business function and can be developed, deployed, and scaled independently. This contrasts with traditional **monolithic architectures**, where all functionality is tightly integrated into a single, large application.

Key Characteristics of Microservices:

1. **Independently Deployable**: Each microservice can be developed, tested, and deployed independently, enabling more frequent releases.

2. **Decentralized Data Management**: Each microservice typically manages its own database or state, ensuring that services are decoupled and can operate independently.

3. **Technology Agnostic**: Different microservices can be written in different programming languages or use

227

different technologies, depending on the specific needs of the service.

4. **Resilience**: Failure in one microservice does not necessarily affect others, allowing the system as a whole to remain functional.

5. **Scalability**: Individual services can be scaled independently based on their specific resource requirements.

Microservices enable better flexibility, scalability, and maintainability for large applications, especially in complex environments where different teams work on different parts of the application.

Why Docker is Ideal for Microservices

Docker is particularly well-suited for managing microservices architectures due to its lightweight, portable, and isolated containerization model. Here are several reasons why Docker is ideal for microservices:

1. Containerization and Isolation

- Each microservice can be packaged into a Docker container, which provides a consistent, isolated environment for the service to run in. This ensures that the service will run the same way in development, testing, and production environments, eliminating compatibility issues.

2. Scalability

- Docker makes it easy to scale individual microservices independently. If a microservice needs more resources due to high traffic, you can scale that specific container without affecting other parts of the application.

3. Rapid Deployment and Continuous Integration

- Docker's fast container startup time makes it ideal for continuous integration and continuous deployment (CI/CD) pipelines, enabling faster development cycles for microservices.
- Docker's portability allows microservices to be deployed quickly across different environments (local, staging, production) without any environment-specific issues.

4. Independent Development and Deployment

- Docker enables teams to develop, test, and deploy microservices independently. Each microservice can be developed using different technologies or frameworks, and Docker ensures that these services can be integrated seamlessly.

229

5. Simplified Management

- Docker, combined with tools like **Docker Compose** and **Docker Swarm**, simplifies the management of multiple containers, making it easier to deploy, scale, and manage microservices across a distributed system.

Designing Microservices with Docker and Docker Compose

Designing microservices with Docker involves breaking down the application into smaller, self-contained services. These services can communicate with each other through APIs or message queues. Docker Compose, which allows you to define and run multi-container Docker applications, is a powerful tool for managing microservices in development environments.

1. Structuring Microservices with Docker

When designing microservices with Docker, the goal is to create independent services that can be developed, deployed, and scaled separately. Each microservice should:

- Have its own **Dockerfile**, which specifies the dependencies, environment, and commands to build the service.
- Be run as a separate Docker container.

- Use **API-based communication** (e.g., REST or gRPC) to interact with other services.

2. Using Docker Compose for Multi-Container Microservices

Docker Compose allows you to define all the microservices in your application, along with their networks, volumes, and configurations, in a single YAML file (`docker-compose.yml`). This makes it easy to spin up and manage multiple microservices at once.

Example `docker-compose.yml` for a microservices-based application:

yaml

```
version: '3'
services:
  web:
    build: ./web
    ports:
      - "8080:8080"
    depends_on:
      - db

  db:
    image: mysql:5.7
    environment:
      MYSQL_ROOT_PASSWORD: example
```

231

```
    volumes:
      - db-data:/var/lib/mysql

    cache:
      image: redis:alpine

  volumes:
    db-data:
```

In this example:

- The **web** service is built from a local `Dockerfile` and exposed on port 8080.
- The **db** service is a MySQL container, which stores its data in a volume (`db-data`).
- The **cache** service uses a Redis image, providing caching for the web service.

The `depends_on` directive ensures that the `web` service is started after the `db` service.

3. Service Communication in Dockerized Microservices

Microservices typically need to communicate with one another. In Docker, services can communicate via Docker networks or directly using service names, which Docker automatically resolves.

For instance, in the `docker-compose.yml` above, the `web` service can access the `db` service by referring to it as `db` (its service name) in the connection string.

Example of connecting to the MySQL database in the `web` service:

```javascript
const mysql = require('mysql');
const connection = mysql.createConnection({
  host: 'db',
  user: 'root',
  password: 'example',
  database: 'mydb'
});
```

This approach eliminates the need for static IP addresses, and Docker ensures that the services are always reachable by their names.

Best Practices for Managing Microservices with Docker

While Docker simplifies the deployment and management of microservices, there are several best practices to follow to ensure scalability, maintainability, and security.

233

1. Maintain Small, Single-Purpose Containers

Each microservice should be encapsulated in a small, focused container. Avoid building large, monolithic Docker images that contain multiple services. Keep each container dedicated to a single service, which aligns with the microservices architecture.

2. Leverage Multi-Stage Builds in Dockerfiles

Multi-stage builds help you reduce the size of Docker images by separating the build environment from the runtime environment. This is particularly useful when your microservices include build-time dependencies that aren't needed at runtime.

Example of a multi-stage Dockerfile:

```
Dockerfile

# Build Stage
FROM node:14 AS build
WORKDIR /app
 . .

RUN npm install
RUN npm run build

# Runtime Stage
FROM node:14-slim
WORKDIR /app
 --from=build /app/dist /app
```

234

```
RUN npm install --production
CMD ["node", "server.js"]
```

3. Version Your Services

Versioning microservices allows you to maintain backward compatibility and manage updates without disrupting existing users. Use semantic versioning ($v1.0.0$, $v1.1.0$, etc.) for each microservice to keep track of changes.

4. Use Environment Variables for Configuration

Store environment-specific configurations (e.g., database credentials, API keys) as environment variables instead of hard-coding them into your Dockerfiles or application code. Docker allows you to easily pass environment variables into containers at runtime using the -e flag or .env files in Docker Compose.

Example of setting environment variables in Docker Compose:

yaml

```
services:
  web:
    build: ./web
    environment:
      - DB_HOST=db
      - DB_USER=root
      - DB_PASSWORD=secret
```

5. Implement Service Discovery

For a large microservices architecture, **service discovery** helps ensure that services can find and communicate with each other dynamically. Docker Swarm and Kubernetes both support service discovery features out of the box, allowing containers to access each other by service names.

6. Ensure Data Persistence

Microservices that require persistent data (e.g., databases) should use Docker volumes for data storage, ensuring that data is preserved across container restarts. Docker Compose makes it easy to define volumes for stateful services.

Example:

yaml

```
db:
  image: mysql:5.7
  environment:
    MYSQL_ROOT_PASSWORD: secret
  volumes:
    - db-data:/var/lib/mysql
```

7. Implement Logging and Monitoring

Microservices require robust logging and monitoring to track the performance and health of individual services. Use tools like

236

Prometheus, **Grafana**, or **ELK/EFK stacks** to aggregate and analyze logs and metrics from multiple containers. Implement centralized logging for better visibility into the entire system.

Summary:

In this chapter, we explored how Docker is an ideal tool for building and managing **microservices architectures**. Docker containers provide the isolation, scalability, and portability needed to effectively develop and deploy microservices. We discussed how to design microservices using Docker and Docker Compose, which allows for the easy management of multi-container applications. Additionally, we outlined best practices for managing microservices with Docker, including maintaining small containers, using environment variables, implementing service discovery, and ensuring data persistence. Docker makes it easy to scale and deploy microservices, allowing development teams to work efficiently and deliver robust, scalable applications.

CHAPTER 23

ADVANCED DOCKER FEATURES AND OPTIMIZATION

Advanced Docker Compose Features (Networks, Dependencies)

Docker Compose simplifies managing multi-container applications, and it offers several advanced features to make your workflows more efficient. These features include managing networks, defining dependencies between services, and more.

1. Custom Networks in Docker Compose

Docker Compose allows you to define custom networks for your services, improving service isolation, communication, and traffic management. By default, all services in a Docker Compose file are attached to a default network, but you can create custom networks to better manage your application's connectivity.

Example of defining a custom network:

```yaml
version: '3'
services:
```

238

```
web:
  image: nginx
  networks:
    - frontend

api:
  image: my-api
  networks:
    - frontend
    - backend

db:
  image: mysql
  networks:
    - backend

networks:
  frontend:
  backend:
```

In this example:

- The `web` and `api` services are connected to the `frontend` network.
- The `api` and `db` services are connected to the `backend` network.
- This setup ensures that the `web` service can communicate with the `api` service, and the `api` service can

communicate with the db service, while isolating networks for better security.

2. Defining Service Dependencies with depends_on

Docker Compose provides the depends_on directive, which ensures that one service starts only after another service is up and running. This is useful when certain services (like databases or message brokers) need to be up and ready before other services can start.

Example:

```yaml
version: '3'
services:
  web:
    image: nginx
    depends_on:
      - api

  api:
    image: my-api
    depends_on:
      - db

  db:
    image: mysql
```

In this case, the `web` service depends on the `api` service, and the `api` service depends on the `db` service. However, note that `depends_on` does not wait for the services to be "ready" (e.g., a database accepting connections); it just ensures the container starts in the correct order.

3. Using Volumes with Docker Compose

Volumes in Docker Compose allow you to persist data between container restarts. Volumes are particularly useful for stateful applications like databases. You can define named volumes in your `docker-compose.yml` file and mount them into the containers.

Example:

```yaml
services:
  db:
    image: mysql
    volumes:
      - db-data:/var/lib/mysql

volumes:
  db-data:
```

In this example, `db-data` is a named volume that ensures that the MySQL database data is persisted even when the container is removed or recreated.

Optimizing Docker Images for Faster Builds

Optimizing Docker images is crucial for improving build times, reducing disk usage, and ensuring faster deployments. Docker images can quickly become large, which impacts both build times and performance. Here are some techniques for optimizing Docker images:

1. Minimize Layers in Dockerfile

Each instruction in a Dockerfile creates a layer in the resulting image. To optimize the size and build time of the image, you should minimize the number of layers and combine multiple commands into a single RUN statement where possible.

Instead of:

```
Dockerfile

RUN apt-get update
RUN apt-get install -y curl
RUN apt-get clean
```

You can combine them into one RUN statement:

```
Dockerfile
```

```
RUN apt-get update && apt-get install -y curl &&
apt-get clean
```

This reduces the number of layers and speeds up the build process.

2. Use Smaller Base Images

Start with smaller base images to reduce the overall image size. **Alpine Linux** is a popular choice for a minimal base image. It's a lightweight, security-focused distribution that contains only the essentials.

Example:

```
Dockerfile
```

```
FROM alpine:latest
```

Using **Alpine** or other minimal base images helps reduce the size of your Docker images and speeds up both the build and deployment processes.

3. Remove Unnecessary Files

After installing dependencies, remove any unnecessary files that aren't required for running the application. For instance, after installing packages, you can delete the package manager's cache.

Example:

```
Dockerfile
```

```
RUN apt-get update && apt-get install -y curl &&
apt-get clean && rm -rf /var/lib/apt/lists/*
```

This ensures that no unnecessary files are left behind in the image, reducing its size.

4. Avoid Installing Unnecessary Dependencies

Only install the dependencies required for your application. Remove any unnecessary packages that are not used at runtime. For example, development dependencies or build tools should be avoided in production images.

Use **multi-stage builds** (discussed below) to install build dependencies in a separate build stage and only the final application into the production image.

Using Multi-Stage Builds for More Efficient Containerization

Multi-stage builds allow you to optimize Docker images by separating the build environment from the runtime environment. In a multi-stage build, you can define multiple FROM statements in the Dockerfile, each creating a separate image stage. This approach allows you to discard intermediate stages that contain unnecessary files or dependencies, resulting in a smaller final image.

How Multi-Stage Builds Work

- **Build Stage**: In the first stage, you compile or build the application, including all the necessary development tools and dependencies.
- **Runtime Stage**: In the second stage, you only the necessary files from the build stage and discard the build dependencies. This results in a minimal runtime image.

Example of a multi-stage Dockerfile:

```
Dockerfile

# Build Stage
FROM node:14 AS build
WORKDIR /app
   . .
RUN npm install
```

```
RUN npm run build

# Runtime Stage
FROM node:14-slim
WORKDIR /app
 --from=build /app/dist /app
RUN npm install --production
CMD ["node", "server.js"]
```

In this example:

- The **build stage** installs dependencies and builds the application.
- The **runtime stage** only copies the necessary files from the build stage (in this case, the `dist` folder) and installs only production dependencies.
- This results in a much smaller image because build tools and development dependencies are not included in the final image.

Benefits of Multi-Stage Builds

- **Smaller Final Image**: Only the files required for the application to run are included in the final image, reducing size.
- **Faster Builds**: By isolating build dependencies from runtime dependencies, the Dockerfile becomes cleaner,

246

and only the necessary files are copied into the final image.

- **Security**: By separating build dependencies, you reduce the attack surface of the final image, as unnecessary tools are not included.

Performance Tuning in Docker Containers

Optimizing the performance of Docker containers is essential for ensuring that your applications run efficiently. Docker provides several ways to tune the performance of containers, including adjusting resource limits, optimizing I/O, and improving networking.

1. Limiting Resource Usage (CPU and Memory)

You can control how much CPU and memory each container uses by setting resource limits. This is useful in production environments to prevent any single container from consuming too many resources and impacting other containers.

Example of limiting CPU and memory:

```bash
docker run --memory="512m" --cpus="1.0" my-container
```

- **Memory Limits**: The `--memory` flag sets the maximum amount of memory the container can use. If the container exceeds this limit, it will be terminated.
- **CPU Limits**: The `--cpus` flag sets the maximum number of CPU cores the container can use.

2. Optimizing Disk I/O

Disk I/O can become a bottleneck if your containerized application performs a lot of read/write operations. Docker allows you to optimize disk I/O by using volume drivers that are optimized for performance.

For example, using a **volume** with optimized storage for database containers can reduce I/O bottlenecks:

```bash

docker volume create --driver local my-db-volume
```

This volume driver ensures optimized read and write operations for stateful applications.

3. Optimizing Network Performance

Containers communicate over the network, and poor network performance can slow down containerized applications. Docker allows you to configure container networking to improve performance.

- **Host Networking**: You can use the host's networking stack for containers by using the `--network host` option. This removes the network isolation between containers and the host, improving performance.

Example:

```bash

docker run --network host my-container
```

- **Dedicated Networks**: Create dedicated networks for your containers to reduce overhead and improve isolation.

```bash

docker network create --driver bridge my-network
```

4. Storage Optimization

If your containerized application uses large amounts of storage, it's important to ensure that your containers are using optimized storage options. Docker volumes are typically faster than bind mounts, and using a dedicated storage driver can help reduce disk I/O bottlenecks.

Summary:

In this chapter, we explored advanced Docker features and optimization techniques. We discussed how to leverage **Docker Compose** for advanced network configurations and service dependencies, optimizing Docker images for faster builds by reducing layers and using smaller base images, and implementing **multi-stage builds** to produce smaller, more efficient container images. Additionally, we covered **performance tuning** in Docker containers, including resource limits for CPU and memory, optimizing disk I/O, and improving network performance. By following these optimization techniques, you can ensure your Docker containers are efficient, scalable, and production-ready.

CHAPTER 24

DOCKER AND SERVERLESS ARCHITECTURES

What is Serverless Computing and How Does Docker Fit In?

Serverless computing is a cloud-native development model where developers can build and run applications without having to manage the underlying infrastructure. In serverless environments, developers only need to focus on writing code, while the cloud provider automatically handles scaling, infrastructure provisioning, and maintenance.

Key Characteristics of Serverless Computing:

- **Event-driven**: Serverless applications are typically event-driven, meaning that functions are executed in response to specific events (e.g., HTTP requests, file uploads, database changes).
- **Automatic Scaling**: Serverless platforms automatically scale resources based on demand. You don't need to manually provision or manage servers.
- **No Server Management**: The server management and maintenance tasks (e.g., patching, scaling) are handled by

the cloud provider, freeing developers from having to manage infrastructure.

- **Pay-as-you-go**: You only pay for the compute resources used during function execution, which can be more cost-effective for certain use cases.

While serverless computing abstracts infrastructure management, it introduces some challenges, particularly with deployment and execution environments. This is where **Docker** can provide value.

How Docker Fits Into Serverless Architectures

Docker allows developers to package applications and services into containers that encapsulate all dependencies and configurations. While serverless platforms typically run individual functions or code snippets, Docker provides a portable, consistent runtime environment. Docker containers can be used in serverless environments to ensure that the code runs in the same way across different environments, from development to testing to production.

Serverless platforms like AWS Lambda, Azure Functions, and Google Cloud Functions traditionally support running code in the form of functions, but **Docker** helps bring more flexibility and control to these environments by packaging entire applications and their dependencies into containers.

Using Docker with Serverless Platforms like AWS Lambda

AWS Lambda is a serverless compute service that runs your code in response to events such as HTTP requests via **API Gateway**, changes to data in **S3**, or updates to a **DynamoDB** table. AWS Lambda natively supports several programming languages (e.g., Python, Node.js, Java), but Docker has brought additional flexibility.

1. Dockerizing AWS Lambda Functions

AWS Lambda now supports running custom Docker images as the execution environment for Lambda functions. This allows you to package your Lambda function and its dependencies into a Docker image and deploy it to Lambda, providing more control over the runtime environment.

- **How Docker Fits into AWS Lambda**:
  - Docker images allow you to run applications and services within a consistent environment. By using Docker with Lambda, you can ensure that your application runs consistently, regardless of where it is deployed (local, development, staging, or production).
  - Dockerizing your Lambda functions gives you the flexibility to use any programming language, library, or toolset inside your container, which

might not be supported by the native Lambda runtimes.

2. Deploying Docker Images to AWS Lambda

To deploy a Docker container to AWS Lambda, you need to create a custom image that meets the Lambda runtime interface. Here's an example workflow:

1. **Create a Dockerfile**:
   - The `Dockerfile` should define the base image, add application code, and set the entry point for Lambda. You need to base the Docker image on the official `amazon/aws-lambda` runtime image.

Example `Dockerfile` for AWS Lambda:

```
Dockerfile

FROM public.ecr.aws/lambda/python:3.8

#  the function code
 app.py ${LAMBDA_TASK_ROOT}

# Install dependencies (if any)
RUN pip install -r requirements.txt

# Set the command to run the function
```

```
CMD ["app.lambda_handler"]
```

2. **Build the Docker Image**:

```bash
docker build -t my-lambda-function .
```

3. **Push the Docker Image to Amazon ECR (Elastic Container Registry)**:
   o You need to push the Docker image to **Amazon ECR** (or another container registry) to make it accessible to AWS Lambda.

```bash
aws ecr create-repository --repository-name my-lambda-function
docker tag my-lambda-function:latest <aws_account_id>.dkr.ecr.<region>.amazonaws.com/my-lambda-function:latest
docker push <aws_account_id>.dkr.ecr.<region>.amazonaws.com/my-lambda-function:latest
```

4. **Create Lambda Function Using the Docker Image**:
   o After pushing the image, you can create an AWS Lambda function using the custom Docker image.

255

```bash
bash

aws lambda create-function --function-name
my-lambda-function \
  --package-type Image \
  --code
ImageUri=<aws_account_id>.dkr.ecr.<region
>.amazonaws.com/my-lambda-function:latest
\
  --role
arn:aws:iam::aws_account_id:role/my-
lambda-role
```

This process lets you run your containerized function in AWS Lambda, with full control over the environment and dependencies.

Benefits and Challenges of Docker in Serverless Environments

Benefits of Docker in Serverless Environments:

1. **Consistency Across Environments**: Docker ensures that your application runs the same way on your local machine, in testing, staging, and production environments. This is particularly useful in serverless architectures, where the runtime environment is often abstracted and can vary across stages.

2. **Flexibility**: Docker allows you to run any application or service that can run in a container, regardless of the

language, libraries, or dependencies. This flexibility makes Docker a good fit for serverless platforms that support custom runtimes (e.g., AWS Lambda).

3. **Portability**: Docker containers are portable, meaning you can easily move and deploy your serverless applications to different cloud providers or hybrid cloud environments.

4. **Advanced Configuration**: Docker gives you fine-grained control over how your application is packaged, configured, and executed, enabling complex configurations that might not be possible with traditional serverless runtimes.

Challenges of Docker in Serverless Environments:

1. **Cold Start Latency**: One of the main challenges of using Docker in serverless environments is the **cold start latency**. When Docker containers are used in serverless platforms like Lambda, the container image has to be pulled from the container registry and initialized, which can take longer than using a built-in runtime. This can impact response times for serverless functions, especially in high-performance use cases.

2. **Resource Overhead**: Docker containers in serverless environments require more resources compared to native runtimes, which may increase the cost and complexity of serverless deployments. Docker images can be large and

might require more CPU and memory, which could affect scalability and cost-efficiency.

3. **Container Management**: Serverless environments abstract away container management, but when Docker containers are used, there's an additional overhead for managing images, containers, and deployment workflows. This complexity can reduce the simplicity that serverless computing promises.

4. **Security Concerns**: Docker images may introduce security risks, especially when using third-party images. It's essential to ensure that images are properly scanned for vulnerabilities and adhere to security best practices.

Real-World Examples of Docker in Serverless Applications

Docker's ability to provide a consistent environment makes it a good fit for several real-world serverless applications. Here are a few examples:

1. Microservices with Serverless Functions

In many modern applications, microservices are implemented using serverless functions, and Docker helps deploy and manage these services. For example, using AWS Lambda with Docker containers to host microservices in different languages (e.g.,

Node.js, Python, Java) allows teams to use the right tools for each microservice while maintaining a consistent deployment pipeline.

2. Data Processing Workflows

Serverless platforms like AWS Lambda can be used to process data streams or files. Docker can be used to package complex data processing workflows into containers, which can then be executed as serverless functions. For example, a Lambda function could be triggered by an S3 file upload and run a Dockerized data processing pipeline to analyze the file.

3. Custom Runtimes in Lambda

Some applications require custom runtimes that aren't supported by native Lambda runtimes (e.g., using specific machine learning libraries or custom software). Docker allows you to create custom runtime environments, which can be deployed on Lambda, providing more flexibility for specialized workloads.

4. Running Legacy Applications in Serverless Environments

In some cases, legacy applications that are not designed for serverless environments can be containerized using Docker. This allows these applications to be deployed and run in a serverless manner without needing to refactor the codebase, bridging the gap between legacy systems and modern serverless architectures.

259

Summary:

In this chapter, we discussed how Docker can fit into **serverless computing architectures** to provide greater flexibility, consistency, and portability. We explored how Docker integrates with platforms like **AWS Lambda** to run custom container images, which helps in managing dependencies, scaling, and deploying serverless applications. We also reviewed the benefits of using Docker in serverless environments, such as consistency and flexibility, alongside challenges like cold start latency, resource overhead, and container management complexities. Finally, we examined real-world examples where Docker is effectively used in serverless applications, including microservices, data processing workflows, custom runtimes, and legacy application deployment. Docker enhances serverless architectures by providing a portable and controlled environment, making it an invaluable tool for modern cloud-native applications.

CHAPTER 25

DOCKER AND CLOUD COMPUTING

How Docker Integrates with Cloud Services (AWS, Azure, GCP)

Docker integrates seamlessly with major cloud service providers, enabling the deployment and scaling of containerized applications in the cloud. Whether you're using **Amazon Web Services (AWS)**, **Microsoft Azure**, or **Google Cloud Platform (GCP)**, Docker allows you to take advantage of cloud-native features and easily deploy containers across these platforms.

1. Docker and AWS Integration

Amazon Web Services (AWS) provides a comprehensive set of services for running Docker containers, including **Elastic Container Service (ECS)**, **Elastic Kubernetes Service (EKS)**, and **AWS Lambda** for serverless deployments.

- **Elastic Container Service (ECS)**: ECS is AWS's fully managed service for running Docker containers at scale. ECS allows you to define tasks and services, and it automatically manages the scheduling, scaling, and orchestration of your containers.

Example: Deploying Docker containers to ECS

```bash
```

```bash
aws ecs create-cluster --cluster-name my-cluster
aws ecs create-service --cluster my-cluster --service-name my-service --task-definition my-task --desired-count 3
```

- **Elastic Kubernetes Service (EKS)**: EKS is a managed Kubernetes service that makes it easy to run Kubernetes clusters on AWS. You can deploy Docker containers to EKS using Kubernetes, which offers powerful orchestration features for large-scale applications.

Example: Deploying Docker containers on EKS using Kubernetes:

```bash
```

```bash
kubectl apply -f deployment.yaml
```

- **AWS Fargate**: Fargate allows you to run Docker containers without managing the underlying infrastructure. It works with both ECS and EKS, providing a serverless compute engine for containers.

2. Docker and Azure Integration

Microsoft Azure offers several container-related services that integrate with Docker, such as **Azure Kubernetes Service (AKS)**, **Azure Container Instances (ACI)**, and **Azure Container Registry (ACR)**.

- **Azure Kubernetes Service (AKS)**: AKS is a fully managed Kubernetes service that makes it easy to deploy and manage Docker containers on Azure. It abstracts away the complexity of Kubernetes management, enabling developers to focus on building applications.

  Example: Deploying a Docker container to AKS:

  bash

  ```
  kubectl apply -f deployment.yaml
  ```

- **Azure Container Instances (ACI)**: ACI allows you to run Docker containers in the cloud without managing virtual machines. It is suitable for running isolated containers for batch jobs or testing environments.

  Example:

263

```
bash
```

```
az container create --resource-group
myResourceGroup --name mycontainer --image
myapp:latest --cpu 1 --memory 1.5
```

- **Azure Container Registry (ACR)**: ACR is a private Docker container registry service where you can store and manage Docker images.

3. Docker and GCP Integration

Google Cloud Platform (GCP) offers tools like **Google Kubernetes Engine (GKE)**, **Google Cloud Run**, and **Google Container Registry (GCR)** to manage Docker containers.

- **Google Kubernetes Engine (GKE)**: GKE is a fully managed Kubernetes service that simplifies running Docker containers at scale. GKE allows you to run containerized applications on GCP with minimal configuration and management.

Example: Deploying a Docker container to GKE:

```
bash
```

```
kubectl apply -f deployment.yaml
```

- **Google Cloud Run**: Cloud Run is a fully managed compute platform for deploying and running Docker containers in a serverless environment. It automatically scales your application based on incoming traffic.

  Example:

  ```bash
  gcloud run deploy my-service --image gcr.io/my-project/my-image
  ```

- **Google Container Registry (GCR)**: GCR is a private container registry for storing Docker images, enabling easy integration with GKE and other GCP services.

Using Docker in Cloud-Native Applications

Cloud-native applications are designed and built to take full advantage of cloud platforms, scalability, and flexibility. Docker plays a significant role in the cloud-native ecosystem by providing a consistent environment for deploying and running microservices in the cloud.

1. Microservices with Docker

Docker makes it easier to build and deploy **microservices** in a cloud-native environment. Each microservice can be packaged in a separate Docker container and deployed to cloud services like AWS ECS, AKS, or GKE. Containers can communicate with each other through service discovery and load balancing, and can be scaled independently.

- **Service Discovery**: Cloud-native applications often rely on service discovery to dynamically discover and connect to other microservices. Docker integrates well with tools like **Consul** or **Istio** to provide service discovery within a containerized environment.

2. Scalability and Resilience

Docker containers can be deployed and scaled on-demand across the cloud infrastructure. By using orchestration tools like **Kubernetes** or **Docker Swarm**, you can automatically scale your microservices based on demand, ensuring high availability and fault tolerance.

- **Auto-scaling**: In cloud-native applications, auto-scaling helps automatically adjust the number of containers based on traffic. Kubernetes and Docker Swarm provide auto-scaling features based on CPU and memory utilization, ensuring your application can handle varying loads without manual intervention.

- **Self-Healing**: Cloud-native applications benefit from Docker's self-healing capabilities. When containers fail or experience issues, Docker orchestrators like Kubernetes can automatically restart or reschedule containers to healthy nodes, ensuring minimal downtime.

3. CI/CD with Docker

Cloud-native applications benefit from **CI/CD (Continuous Integration and Continuous Deployment)** pipelines. Docker enables efficient CI/CD workflows by creating a consistent, portable environment for building, testing, and deploying applications. Docker images can be built, tested, and deployed in cloud environments using CI/CD platforms like Jenkins, GitLab CI, or GitHub Actions.

Deploying Docker Containers on Kubernetes in the Cloud

Kubernetes is one of the most powerful tools for managing Docker containers at scale in cloud environments. Cloud platforms like AWS, Azure, and GCP provide fully managed Kubernetes services, such as **Amazon EKS**, **Azure AKS**, and **Google GKE**. These services allow you to deploy, manage, and scale Docker containers in production environments.

1. Setting Up Kubernetes Cluster in the Cloud

Each cloud provider offers a managed Kubernetes service that simplifies setting up and managing clusters:

- **AWS EKS**: Amazon's managed Kubernetes service.
- **Azure AKS**: Azure's managed Kubernetes service.
- **Google GKE**: Google's managed Kubernetes service.

To deploy Docker containers on Kubernetes, you first need to create a Kubernetes cluster in your chosen cloud platform and then define deployment configurations (in YAML format) for your containers.

2. Deploying Docker Containers with Kubernetes

Once your Kubernetes cluster is set up, you can deploy Docker containers using Kubernetes deployments, services, and pods. Here is an example of deploying a Docker container on Kubernetes:

1. **Create a Deployment YAML File**: Example `deployment.yaml` for deploying a web application:

yaml

```
apiVersion: apps/v1
kind: Deployment
metadata:
```

```
      name: web-app
spec:
  replicas: 3
  selector:
    matchLabels:
      app: web-app
  template:
    metadata:
      labels:
        app: web-app
    spec:
      containers:
        - name: web
          image: my-web-app:latest
          ports:
            - containerPort: 80
```

2. **Deploy to Kubernetes**:

```bash
bash
```

```
kubectl apply -f deployment.yaml
```

3. **Expose the Application with a Service**: To expose the application outside the Kubernetes cluster, you can create a service that acts as a load balancer:

```bash
bash
```

```
kubectl    expose    deployment    web-app    --
type=LoadBalancer --name=web-app-service
```

Best Practices for Cloud Deployments

When deploying Docker containers in cloud environments, there are several best practices to follow to ensure high availability, scalability, and security.

1. Use Managed Services

Whenever possible, use managed services like **AWS EKS**, **Azure AKS**, or **Google GKE** to handle the complexity of running Kubernetes clusters. These services abstract away the need to manage the underlying infrastructure and provide features like automated scaling, load balancing, and updates.

2. Automate Scaling and Failover

Set up auto-scaling for your containerized applications to ensure that your services can handle traffic spikes and scale down during low demand. Configure **health checks** to ensure that failed containers are automatically replaced with healthy ones.

3. Use Infrastructure-as-Code (IaC)

Define your cloud infrastructure using **Infrastructure-as-Code** tools like **Terraform** or **CloudFormation**. This makes it easier to

270

manage and reproduce your infrastructure across environments, ensuring consistency and minimizing human error.

4. Monitor and Log Your Applications

Set up comprehensive **monitoring** and **logging** systems for your Docker containers in the cloud. Use cloud-native tools like **Amazon CloudWatch, Azure Monitor**, or **Google Stackdriver**, or integrate with open-source solutions like **Prometheus** and **Grafana** to monitor your containers' performance, health, and resource usage.

5. Implement Security Best Practices

Secure your Docker containers by:

- Running containers as non-root users.
- Using private container registries (e.g., **Amazon ECR, Azure Container Registry, Google Container Registry**).
- Scanning images for vulnerabilities using tools like **Clair** or **Trivy**.
- Using **IAM roles** and **RBAC** (Role-Based Access Control) to control access to your cloud resources and Kubernetes cluster.

Summary:

In this chapter, we explored how Docker integrates with major cloud services such as **AWS**, **Azure**, and **GCP**. Docker fits seamlessly into **cloud-native applications**, enabling the deployment of containerized microservices with easy scalability and management. We discussed how to deploy Docker containers on **Kubernetes** in the cloud, making it easier to scale and manage containerized applications. Finally, we covered best practices for cloud deployments, including using managed services, automating scaling, implementing security, and monitoring applications for high availability and performance. By following these practices, you can optimize the deployment and operation of Docker containers in cloud environments, ensuring your applications are scalable, secure, and efficient.

CHAPTER 26

TROUBLESHOOTING DOCKER IN PRODUCTION

Handling Production Issues in Dockerized Apps

Production environments present unique challenges due to the complexity, scale, and critical nature of the applications running. When Dockerized applications run in production, issues can arise related to container performance, resource allocation, networking, or service failures. Effective troubleshooting is crucial to maintaining the availability and performance of the application.

1. Understanding Common Docker Production Issues

Here are some common issues that may arise in production environments:

- **Container Crashes**: Containers can crash due to resource exhaustion (e.g., CPU, memory), application bugs, or misconfigurations.
- **Networking Issues**: Misconfigured network settings or firewall rules can prevent containers from communicating with each other or with external services.

273

- **Resource Exhaustion**: Containers may consume too much CPU, memory, or disk space, causing the host system to become unstable.
- **Configuration Errors**: Misconfigured environment variables, mount points, or volumes can cause containers to fail or behave unexpectedly.
- **Service Failures**: A microservice in a Dockerized app might fail, leading to downtime or partial availability.

2. Best Practices for Troubleshooting Docker in Production

- **Reproduce Locally**: The first step is to try to reproduce the issue in a local or staging environment. This helps to identify if the issue is related to Docker, the application itself, or the infrastructure.
- **Isolate the Problem**: Narrow down whether the issue is with the application, the Docker container, or the underlying infrastructure (e.g., CPU, memory, disk).
- **Consult Docker Logs**: Docker provides logs for containers, which are invaluable for diagnosing issues in production. By inspecting the logs, you can often pinpoint the root cause of an issue.

Logging and Monitoring in Live Environments

Effective logging and monitoring are essential for maintaining the health of Dockerized applications in production. These practices help in identifying, diagnosing, and resolving issues quickly.

1. Docker Logging Mechanisms

Docker offers several logging drivers that allow you to capture logs from your containers and store them for analysis.

- **Default Logging Driver (`json-file`)**: The default logging driver stores logs in JSON format on the host filesystem. You can access these logs with the `docker logs` command.

  Example of viewing logs for a running container:

  ```bash
  bash

  docker logs <container_name_or_id>
  ```

- **Other Logging Drivers**: You can configure Docker to use other logging drivers like **syslog, fluentd, gelf**, or **awslogs**, depending on your logging infrastructure.

Example of running a container with the syslog driver:

```bash
bash
```

275

```
docker run --log-driver=syslog my-container
```

2. Centralized Logging

In a production environment, centralized logging systems like the **ELK stack (Elasticsearch, Logstash, Kibana)** or **EFK stack (Elasticsearch, Fluentd, Kibana)** help you aggregate logs from all containers and services into a single location. These systems allow you to search, visualize, and analyze logs to diagnose issues in real-time.

- **Elasticsearch** stores the logs.
- **Logstash** or **Fluentd** collects and aggregates logs from various sources.
- **Kibana** provides a web interface for searching and visualizing the logs.

3. Monitoring Tools for Docker

Monitoring your Dockerized applications is essential for tracking resource usage (CPU, memory, disk) and ensuring that containers are healthy and performing well.

Popular monitoring tools include:

- **Prometheus**: Collects metrics from Docker containers and other services, storing them in a time-series database.

- **Grafana**: Integrates with Prometheus to visualize metrics in real-time dashboards.

- **cAdvisor**: A Google-developed tool that provides detailed performance metrics for containers.

- **Datadog**: A third-party service that provides container monitoring, log management, and analytics.

4. Real-Time Alerts

Set up alerting systems that notify you of performance issues, such as high CPU or memory usage, or container crashes. Tools like **Prometheus Alertmanager**, **Datadog**, and **New Relic** can send alerts via email, Slack, or other messaging systems when performance thresholds are exceeded.

How to Quickly Fix Common Production Issues

In production, it's crucial to be able to quickly diagnose and resolve issues to minimize downtime. Here are some common production issues and how to address them.

1. Container Crashes

Container crashes are a common issue in production. Common causes include memory exhaustion, application errors, or missing dependencies.

- **Solution**: Use `docker logs <container_name>` to view the logs and determine the cause of the crash. If the issue is memory-related, you may need to adjust resource limits or optimize the application. If the application fails due to missing dependencies, check the Dockerfile for completeness and review the container image.

```bash
docker logs <container_name_or_id>
```

2. High CPU or Memory Usage

If a container is consuming too much CPU or memory, it can affect the performance of the host system and other containers.

- **Solution**: Use `docker stats` to monitor resource usage for all containers in real-time. If a container is using too many resources, you may need to limit its CPU or memory usage using the `--memory` and `--cpus` flags.

Example of limiting memory and CPU:

```bash
docker run --memory="512m" --cpus="1.0" my-container
```

If the issue is related to a memory leak or inefficiency in the application, consider optimizing the application or using profiling tools to identify the cause.

3. Networking Issues

Containers may fail to communicate with each other or external services due to networking misconfigurations.

- **Solution**: Check if the containers are connected to the correct network using `docker network ls`. Use `docker inspect <container_name>` to verify the network configuration and ensure that containers can resolve each other by name.

bash

```
docker network ls
docker inspect <container_name_or_id>
```

If using Docker Compose, ensure that all services are correctly defined in the `docker-compose.yml` file and connected to the appropriate networks.

4. Volume and Storage Issues

Stateful applications may experience issues with volumes, such as missing or inaccessible data.

- **Solution**: Use `docker volume ls` to list all volumes and check if the correct volume is mounted to the container. Ensure that the correct file permissions are set for mounted directories or volumes, especially if the container needs to read or write data.

bash

```
docker volume ls
docker volume inspect <volume_name>
```

For issues with databases or persistent data, ensure that volumes are correctly backed up and restored during maintenance or scaling operations.

Ensuring High Availability and Reliability in Dockerized Apps

High availability and reliability are essential for production applications. Docker provides several features and strategies to ensure that your applications are highly available and resilient to failure.

1. Redundancy and Replication

To ensure high availability, deploy multiple replicas of your services. In **Docker Swarm** or **Kubernetes**, you can easily scale services by increasing the number of replicas.

280

- **Docker Swarm**: Use the `docker service scale` command to increase the number of replicas for a service.

```bash
```

```bash
docker service scale web=3
```

- **Kubernetes**: Use the `kubectl scale` command to scale the number of pods.

```bash
```

```bash
kubectl scale deployment my-web-app --replicas=3
```

2. Load Balancing

Use **load balancing** to distribute traffic across multiple instances of a service. Docker Swarm and Kubernetes both offer built-in load balancing, and you can also use external tools like **NGINX** or **Traefik** to handle load balancing.

In **Docker Swarm**, load balancing is automatically handled when you expose a service via a port:

```bash
```

```bash
docker service create --name web --replicas 3 -p 8080:80 nginx
```

281

In **Kubernetes**, you can create a service to expose your application and distribute traffic across the available pods.

3. Health Checks

Docker provides the ability to define **health checks** for containers, which ensures that only healthy containers receive traffic. By using HEALTHCHECK in the Dockerfile or defining it in the Docker Compose or Kubernetes configurations, you can automatically restart containers that are not functioning correctly.

Example Dockerfile health check:

```
Dockerfile

HEALTHCHECK    --interval=5m    --timeout=3s    --
retries=3 \
  CMD  curl  --fail  http://localhost:8080/health
|| exit 1
```

In Kubernetes, you can define liveness and readiness probes to monitor container health and readiness to receive traffic.

4. Service Discovery and Load Balancing

For multi-container applications, use **service discovery** to ensure that containers can dynamically find and communicate with each other. Docker Swarm and Kubernetes offer built-in service discovery, where containers can reference other services by their

282

name (e.g., `web`, `db`), and the orchestrator automatically resolves the service to the appropriate container.

Summary:

In this chapter, we discussed best practices for **troubleshooting Dockerized applications in production**, including handling common production issues such as container crashes, resource exhaustion, networking problems, and storage issues. We covered how to **log and monitor** your containers in live environments, using tools like `docker logs`, `docker stats`, and integrated monitoring solutions such as **Prometheus** and **Grafana**. We also explored strategies for ensuring **high availability** and **reliability**, such as using redundancy, load balancing, health checks, and service discovery in Docker Swarm and Kubernetes. By applying these practices, you can maintain the stability, performance, and resilience of Dockerized applications in production.

CHAPTER 27

THE FUTURE OF DOCKER AND CONTAINERIZATION

The Evolution of Docker and Container Technology

Docker revolutionized the way developers and system administrators approach application deployment by introducing the concept of containerization. Prior to Docker, applications were typically deployed on physical or virtual machines, often leading to dependency issues and inconsistencies across development, staging, and production environments. Docker solved these problems by encapsulating applications and their dependencies into lightweight, portable containers, ensuring that they run consistently in any environment.

1. Docker's Early Years (2013-2015)

Docker was first introduced in 2013, and its impact was immediate. It offered a solution to the "works on my machine" problem by allowing applications to run consistently across different environments. Docker containers were initially built on top of **LXC (Linux Containers)** but later evolved into their own

284

technology, using the **Docker Engine** to create, manage, and run containers.

- **Docker Hub**: In 2013, Docker introduced **Docker Hub**, a centralized registry where users could share and distribute Docker images. This made it easier for developers to access pre-configured container images for common services like databases, web servers, and more.
- **Docker Compose**: In 2014, Docker introduced **Docker Compose**, a tool that allowed developers to define multi-container applications in a single YAML file, making it easier to work with complex applications.

2. Expanding Ecosystem (2016-2018)

During this period, Docker's ecosystem expanded significantly. The introduction of **Docker Swarm** for container orchestration allowed Docker users to manage clusters of containers natively within the Docker toolset.

- **Docker Swarm and Kubernetes**: As Kubernetes emerged as the dominant orchestration platform for containerized applications, Docker started integrating Kubernetes into its ecosystem. Kubernetes was adopted as the standard orchestration tool for large-scale, cloud-native applications due to its extensive features like automatic scaling, self-healing, and advanced networking.

- **Container Registries and Security**: With the growth of container adoption, Docker focused on security and introduced features like **Docker Content Trust** and **Docker Scan** to help users identify vulnerabilities in their images. Additionally, container registries like **AWS ECR**, **Google Container Registry**, and **Azure Container Registry** became popular for storing Docker images securely.

3. Docker Today (2019-Present)

In recent years, Docker has evolved to support a wider range of deployment use cases, from local development to large-scale cloud environments. Docker's ability to integrate with cloud services and container orchestration platforms like Kubernetes has solidified its place in modern DevOps practices.

- **Docker Desktop and Docker for Windows/Mac**: Docker made it easier for developers to run containers on their local machines with **Docker Desktop**, which supports both **Windows** and **Mac** environments.
- **Docker as a Service**: Docker is increasingly offered as a service by cloud providers. Docker's integration with **Amazon ECS, Google Kubernetes Engine (GKE)**, and

Azure Kubernetes Service (AKS) makes it easier to deploy and manage containers in the cloud.

As we move forward, Docker continues to improve its tooling, user experience, and security features, keeping it a central player in the containerization and DevOps space.

Trends in Container Orchestration and Management

Container orchestration is key to managing containerized applications at scale. Docker's integration with orchestration tools like **Kubernetes**, **Docker Swarm**, and **Apache Mesos** has made it easier to automate the deployment, scaling, and management of containers in both on-premises and cloud environments. The future of container orchestration is marked by several key trends:

1. Kubernetes Dominance

Kubernetes has rapidly become the de facto standard for container orchestration due to its robust features and active open-source community. It offers advanced scheduling, scaling, and self-healing capabilities, making it ideal for complex, cloud-native applications.

- **Unified Orchestration and Management**: Kubernetes is expanding beyond container orchestration to include management of other resources such as storage and

287

networking. Kubernetes is increasingly being used to manage **stateful applications** (e.g., databases) alongside stateless services like microservices.

- **Serverless Containers with Kubernetes**: With tools like **Knative**, Kubernetes is being extended to support serverless applications. Knative allows developers to run containerized workloads on Kubernetes without managing the underlying infrastructure, combining the benefits of containers with the simplicity of serverless computing.

2. Simplified Orchestration with Docker Compose

While Kubernetes is dominant in large-scale environments, **Docker Compose** remains popular for smaller-scale applications and development environments. Docker Compose is being extended to handle more advanced use cases, such as service discovery, environment variable management, and integration with Kubernetes.

- **Docker Compose and Kubernetes**: Docker Compose files can be converted into Kubernetes manifests using tools like **Kompose**, making it easier to move from local development to production environments.

3. Hybrid and Multi-Cloud Environments

As organizations adopt multi-cloud and hybrid cloud strategies, managing containerized applications across different cloud providers has become a key challenge. Tools like **Red Hat OpenShift** and **Google Anthos** provide a unified platform for managing Kubernetes clusters across multiple clouds, helping to avoid vendor lock-in.

- **Multi-Cloud Orchestration**: Kubernetes is at the heart of multi-cloud strategies, enabling organizations to deploy applications across different cloud providers while maintaining a unified management layer.

The Role of Docker in the Broader DevOps Ecosystem

Docker plays a central role in the **DevOps** ecosystem by enabling consistent and reproducible environments from development through to production. Docker's containerization technology allows developers and operations teams to collaborate more effectively, streamline workflows, and automate tasks.

1. DevOps Automation

Docker is a critical tool for automating the continuous integration and continuous deployment (CI/CD) pipeline. Docker containers can be easily integrated into CI/CD systems like **Jenkins**, **GitLab**

CI, and **GitHub Actions**, ensuring consistent and fast deployments.

- **Automated Testing and Deployment**: Docker ensures that testing environments mirror production environments, allowing for more reliable automated tests. After testing, Docker images can be deployed to production systems using automated deployment pipelines.

2. Containerized Development Environments

Docker simplifies the creation of containerized development environments that are consistent across teams and stages. Developers can package their application along with its dependencies into a Docker image and share it with other developers, ensuring that everyone is working with the same environment.

- **Docker for Local Development**: Docker's ability to run locally and on remote cloud environments makes it an ideal solution for both local development and testing. It enables developers to easily spin up isolated environments for different parts of their application, allowing them to work on individual services without worrying about conflicts.

290

3. Infrastructure as Code (IaC)

Docker integrates well with **Infrastructure as Code** (IaC) practices, enabling infrastructure to be defined and managed programmatically. Tools like **Terraform** and **Ansible** can provision and configure Docker containers, allowing infrastructure to be managed alongside application code.

The Future of Microservices and Containerization

The adoption of **microservices architecture** has accelerated in recent years, and containerization has become the de facto standard for deploying microservices. Docker and Kubernetes provide an ideal foundation for building, managing, and scaling microservices applications, and their future will likely be shaped by the following trends:

1. Serverless Containers

Serverless computing continues to gain traction, and Docker's role in serverless environments will evolve. **Serverless containers** allow organizations to run containerized workloads without managing infrastructure, simplifying deployment and scaling.

- **Knative and AWS Fargate**: These services allow you to run containers in a serverless manner, automatically scaling the number of containers based on demand. As serverless containers become more popular, Docker will continue to play an important role in running microservices without the need to manage underlying infrastructure.

2. Advanced Service Mesh Integration

As microservices applications grow in complexity, **service meshes** like **Istio** and **Linkerd** are becoming crucial for managing communication between services. These tools provide features like load balancing, service discovery, and security within microservices architectures.

- **Containerized Service Mesh**: Docker and Kubernetes will continue to evolve in concert with service mesh technologies to provide a seamless experience for managing microservices at scale.

3. Edge Computing and IoT

As more devices become connected to the internet, **edge computing** (processing data closer to the devices) will become more important. Docker's lightweight nature makes it ideal for running containers on edge devices that need to process data locally before sending it to the cloud.

- **Edge Computing with Docker**: Docker containers will be deployed on edge devices, enabling low-latency processing and efficient resource utilization in Internet of Things (IoT) environments.

4. Enhanced Security for Containers

Security remains a critical concern for containerized environments, and Docker will continue to focus on providing more robust security features to meet the needs of enterprise applications. Features like **Docker Content Trust**, **User Namespaces**, and **AppArmor** profiles will evolve to address the increasing security demands in containerized environments.

Summary:

In this chapter, we explored the **evolution of Docker and container technology**, tracing its journey from a development tool to a central component in cloud-native architectures and DevOps workflows. We discussed the **trends in container orchestration**, with Kubernetes continuing to dominate the space, and the growing importance of Docker in **cloud-native applications**. We also explored Docker's central role in the **DevOps ecosystem**, automating CI/CD pipelines and providing consistent, containerized development environments. Finally, we looked at the future of **microservices and containerization**, including the rise of serverless containers, edge computing, and the need for stronger security measures. Docker's continued evolution and integration with modern technologies will ensure its place at the forefront of containerization and cloud computing for years to come.